# Colonial Reports
# on
# Pakistan's Frontier
# Tribal Areas

# Colonial Reports
# on
# Pakistan's Frontier
# Tribal Areas

Edited and Introduced by

Robert Nichols

OXFORD
UNIVERSITY PRESS

# OXFORD
UNIVERSITY PRESS

Great Clarendon Street, Oxford OX2 6DP

Oxford University Press is a department of the University of Oxford.
It furthers the University's objective of excellence in research, scholarship,
and education by publishing worldwide in

Oxford New York

Auckland Cape Town Dar es Salaam Hong Kong Karachi
Kuala Lumpur Madrid Melbourne Mexico City Nairobi
New Delhi Shanghai Taipei Toronto

with offices in

Argentina Austria Brazil Chile Czech Republic France Greece
Guatemala Hungary Italy Japan South Korea Poland Portugal
Singapore Switzerland Thailand Turkey Ukraine Vietnam

Oxford is a registered trade mark of Oxford University Press
in the UK and in certain other countries

ISBN-13: 978-0-19-547081-9
ISBN-10: 0-19-547081-8

Maps reprinted from *The Pathans: With an Epilogue on Russia*
by Sir Olaf Caroe (Oxford University Press), 1983

Typeset in Times
Printed in Pakistan by
Challenger Paper Product, Karachi.
Published by
Ameena Saiyid, Oxford University Press
Plot No. 38, Sector 15, Korangi Industrial Area, PO Box 8214
Karachi-74900, Pakistan.

# Contents

# Acknowledgements

The editor wishes to acknowledge the support received over several years from colleagues in Peshawar, including Zahir Ullah, Director of the NWFP Library; Muqarrab Khan, Research Officer, NWFP Archives; Shah Murad Khan, Head Librarian, NWFP Library; Ihsan Ali, University of Peshawar and Directorate of Archaeology and Archives, NWFP; and Azmat Hayat Khan of the Area Studies Centre, University of Peshawar. He also wishes to thank Aziza Shahid and Adnan Khan. Finally, many thanks to Ameena Saiyid, Rehana Khandwalla, and all the staff at Oxford University Press.

# Introduction

By October 2003 the Pakistan government faced increased pressure from the United States and the Karzai government of Afghanistan to use military force to pursue border region militants. Taliban and Al-Qaeda fighters contributed to instability in Afghanistan almost two years after the fall of the Taliban government in Afghanistan.

The government of Pakistan was confronted with several problems. The border region was indirectly administered as a series of Federally Administered Tribal Areas. These were culturally, economically, and politically semi-autonomous geographic regions only tenuously supervised by the nation-state through a lightly revised British colonial structure of political agents, subsidies, and coercive, often collective, politics and punishments. This structure dated to Frontier Crimes Regulations introduced as early as 1872.

Also, in 2004 the North West Frontier Province adjoining the several FATA territories was ruled by the MMA coalition of Islamist political parties that had swept the NWFP provincial elections in October 2002. These parties had opposed the US war in Afghanistan and had many members in the provincial and national assembly who were allies of, even teachers of, many of the Taliban and their foreign supporters. Finally, the President of Pakistan, Pervez Musharraf continued to rule under extreme pressure from domestic Islamist political groups demanding he not turn his back on years of state support for Islamist agendas in Kashmir and Afghanistan. Negotiations between the government and border clans continued throughout the winter of 2003–4. By spring 2004, ongoing violence in both Iraq and Afghanistan led to increased political pressure on Islamabad. The Pakistan government was forced to move beyond a series of protracted negotiations with FATA clan leaders. Pakistan forces had been able to occupy areas of the Mohmand Agency up to the 'Durand Line' border. But little movement had been made towards eliminating the many hundreds of refugee Taliban and Al-Qaeda figures settled in the rugged and isolated Pakistan border areas of North and South Waziristan. In contrast to periodic US search-and-destroy sweeps along the Afghan side of the border, in April 2004 the Pakistan government chose to intensify the use of political tools first tested by the British a century earlier.

Local clan leaders and self-chosen or government appointed councils or *jirgas* negotiated a settlement meant to avoid direct conflict with gathering Pakistani military forces. The April 2004 Shakai agreement allowed and required tribal militias to disperse the Al-Qaeda supporters. Five wanted local Pashtun activists were to surrender and receive amnesty in return for pledges of good conduct. Foreigners would not be arrested, but were required to register with the government and abstain from further militancy. Many Arabs and Central Asians were scattered in the region. The press commonly estimated 500-600. Some were long settled in the area in exile from home countries. Many had married into local communities after the fall of the communist government in Kabul or after the fall of the Taliban. Some undoubtedly continued to return periodically to action in Afghanistan.

The Shakai agreement failed. No militants registered with the government. On 30 May 2004, Asmatullah Gandapur, the political agent for South Waziristan, ordered collective punishment against the Ahmedzai Wazirs in and around Wana town. Up to 5,500 shops and businesses were ordered closed. Two hundred or more truckloads of produce (including tomatoes and peaches) and up to one hundred twenty truckloads of apples were reported banned from movement to markets. In June, the outspoken rhetoric of Nek Mohammad, a Yargulkhel clan leader who had fought with the Taliban, ensured renewed confrontations, dozens of casualties, and thousands of refugees from the Wana area. Nek Mohammad had negotiated and agreed to the April truce, then denied the requirements to register non-Pashtuns and refrain from jihad. He was targeted by the military and killed. Hundreds, perhaps thousands, attended his funeral.

The government continued an economic embargo in Wana into mid-July. Afghan refugee camps were cleared, the residents forced back to Afghanistan or out of the area. Thousands of shops remained closed. The military occupied key valley areas and attacked militants in surrounding hills. Islamist and tribal fighters ambushed vehicles, mortared and shelled government centres and bases. The government action offended Pashtunwali social codes offering shelter to guests, especially those married into local families. Militants threatened and launched attacks further afield, including a dramatic 9 June attack in Karachi on a leading Pakistan Army general. Sporadic rocket attacks continued on towns, including Tank in D.I. Khan district. Near Wana, the Frontier Corps continued ground attacks and artillery barrages in the hills north of the Shakai valley.

Some political movement came on 19 July 2004. The Ahmedzai Wazir *jirga* surrendered twenty-seven members of the Karmazkhel and Malikkhel clans wanted by the political administration. The men included four religious leaders. The two most wanted figures, Maulavi Abbas and Commander Javed Karmazkhel, and others on an original list of forty-four names, remained at large.

Nominally a key moment in the US 'war on terrorism', the summer offensive in South Waziristan represented a more familiar FATA pattern of conflict. As in the British period, it was confrontation marked by limited state authority, colourful often symbolic political theatre, and a less obvious process of sustained and incremental negotiation and coalition building. Casualties were real, but low-grade guerrilla warfare was more certain than any final resolution.

Of interest to the historian are recurring names and themes from previous generations of state-building activity along a borderland that once divided and vexed empires and now divided two struggling nation-states. In 2004, the Ahmadzai Wazir around Wana town, including their Zalikhel sub-clan and the Yargulkhel sub-lineage of the Zalikhel, suffered economic blockade, destruction of family homes, and manipulation from political agents to force their cooperation in dealing with foreign and domestic militants in the Ahmedzai Wazir homelands. As in the nineteenth century, religious sentiment and rhetoric stoked clan-based resistance to state intrusions and demands. As in earlier moments of confrontation after independence in 1947, Pakistan leaders talked of bringing development, modernization, and the rule of law to the tribal areas. Towns and villages, such as Wana and Azam Warsak, and locations such as the Shakai valley were names from earlier decades of conflict, punishment, and state intrusion into areas not yet fully encapsulated into state ideologies and systems.

A century earlier, colonial officials had periodically generated secret reports to build a record of the accumulated compromises, subsidies, and personal relationships established by British political agents asked to control the FATA regions. Post-colonial scholars have recovered several of these reports, listed in the bibliography, to gain insight in colonial political policies and glean social and cultural material about the 'tribal' Pashtun societies of the FATA territories. Colonial reports on the Mahsuds, the Orakzai, and the Mohmand have been published and studied. Others remain in old files and archives to be studied and recovered.

The ideas and imagery contained in such documents, complete with nineteenth century imperial and Orientalist cultural and political biases, have too often been simply recycled by post-colonial authorities and the occasional scholar drawn to narratives that reinforce state agendas and social and cultural hierarchies. Nevertheless, such reports remain fascinating historical archives of local data and imperial mentalities.

This short volume contains two colonial reports written a few years after the sustained unrest of the 1897–8 period. In this period, large and frequent colonial punitive expeditions were launched to suppress border resistance against British encroachments into autonomous Pashtun and northern border regions. In 1901, attempting to better control the region, the British consolidated these complex trans-Indus politics and territories into a new North-West Frontier Province.

The confidential report *Notes on Wana* was written in 1903 and printed for the education of future political agents. The political agent/author wrote his essay in the wake of fifteen years or more of local colonial political interventions. These included an 1895 military expedition against regional Mahsud clans, a blockade against the Mahsuds from 1895 to 1901, and a subsequent reorganization of the complex distribution pattern of subsidies among the leadership of the many lineages. These subsidies were intended to produce a group of loyal *maliks* and headmen who might be used to spread government influence among their villages and clans. More typically, as was evidenced in the summer of 2004, officially supported leaders, and officially appointed councils, meant little without overall negotiation and consensus among all the concerned clans and individuals.

The second report, *Notes on the Adam Khel Afridis*, was written in 1901. The Adam Khel Afridis, famous for an indigenous arms industry, dominated the Kohat Pass route south of Peshawar. Their ability to hinder or help strategic communications meant that they received the first of the many British subsidies that would be paid to border clans after the 1849 British occupation of the Punjab and the trans-Indus districts. This report, similar to the Wana report, is a mixture of political history, ethnographic detail, personal experience and interpretation, and tribal folklore and genealogy. Discussed are aspects of geography and routes as well as fine details of political settlements and financial subsidies. Strategies of control are elaborated upon, including pressure when necessary on the local salt trade.

On 20 July 2004, the Pakistani newspaper the *International News* detailed the negotiations that continued in the Wana region. The Pakistani nation-state needed to both achieve results for foreign allies and maintain legitimacy with local populations. The tools deployed were less from the war of terrorism than from a century of colonial and post-colonial strategies of coercion, accommodation, and patient, often futile, divide and rule tactics,

> ...The administration has given another option to the tribes either to present one person each per family from both the sub-tribes in case Javed and Abbas refuse to surrender or face demolition of six houses of each of the tribe as punishment for defying the government orders....

Into August, government ground attacks, air strikes, and artillery barrages continued in the region in response to militant ambushes and rocket attacks. The collective punishment of shop and road closings was lifted for ten days, then re-imposed as *jirgas* failed to meet government demands.

Those interested in the possibility of understanding continued conflict and violence along the Pakistan-Afghanistan border will gain some insight from the series of earlier, colonial reports. They reflected the assertions of a powerful government able to accumulate systematic knowledge about specific regional populations as that government claimed the right to regulate and control local politics and behaviour. Importantly, the reports also reflected the limits of such claims about knowledge and authority. In both the colonial and post-colonial periods, modern state power often developed in advance of the ability of a government to gain full legitimacy and cooperation among populations yet to be fully integrated into wider economic, legal, and administrative systems.

## Partial bibliography of relevant published reports and literature in English

Ahmed, Akbar S., *Millennium and Charisma Among Pathans: An Essay in Social Anthropology*, Routledge and Kegan Paul, London, 1976.

Ahmed, Akbar S., *Social and Economic Change in the Tribal Areas, 1972–1976*, Oxford University Press, Karachi, 1977.

Barth, Fredrik, and Miangul Jahanzeb, *The Last Wali of Swat, An Autobiography*, reprint, Orchid Press, Bangkok, 1995.

Barth, Fredrik, *Political Leadership Among Swat Pathans*, reprint, Athone Press, New Jersey, 1965.

Beattie, Hugh, *Imperial Frontier: Tribe and State in Waziristan*, Routledge, 2001.

Bellew, H. W., *A General Report on the Yusufzai*, 1864, reprint, Sang-e-Meel Publications, Lahore, 1994.

Caroe, Olaf, *The Pathans, 550 BC-AD 1957, 1958*, reprint, Oxford University Press, Karachi, 1992.

Donald, D., *Notes on the Adam Khel Afridis*, Punjab Government Press, Lahore, 1901.

Elphinstone, Mountstuart, *An Account of the Kingdom of Caubul*, London, 2 vols., 1815, reprint, Indus Publications, Karachi, 1992.

Grima, Benedicte, *The Performance of Emotion Among Paxtun Women*, Oxford University Press, Karachi, 1993.

Howell, E., *Mizh: A Monograph on Government's Relations with the Mahsud Tribe*, 1931, reprint, Oxford University Press, Karachi, 1979.

Ibbetson, Denzil and Edward Maclagan, compiled by H. A. Rose, *Glossary of the Tribes and Castes of the Punjab and NWFP*, vol. III, reprint, 1978.

Johnston, F. W., *Notes on Wana (Recorded in 1903)*.

Khan, Muhammad Hayat, *Hayat-i-Afghani*, 1865, translated by Henry Priestley as *Afghanistan and Its Inhabitants*, Rookun-ud-din, 1874, reprint, Sang-e-Meel Publications, Lahore, 1981.

King, L. W., *Monograph on the Orakzai Country and Clans*, Punjab Government Press, Lahore, 1900.

Lindholm, Charles, *Frontier Perspectives: Essays in Comparative Anthropology*, Oxford University Press, Karachi, 1996.

Lindholm, Charles, *Generosity and Jealousy: The Swat Pakhtun of Northern Pakistan*, Columbia University Press, New York, 1982.

Merk, W. R. H., *Report on the Mohmands*, 1898, reprint, Vanguard, Lahore, 1984.

Mohmand, Sher Muhammad, *FATA: A Socio-Cultural and Geo-Political History*, no publisher, no date, purchased at the Saeed Book Bank in Peshawar, 2004.

Nichols, Robert, *Settling the Frontier: Land, Law and Society in the Peshawar Valley, 1500–1900*, Oxford University Press, Karachi, 2001.

Neamet Ullah, *Makhzan-i-Afghanistan*, translated by Bernhard Dorn, *History of the Afghans*, reprint, Karachi, 1976.

Noelle, Christine, *State and Tribe in Nineteenth-Century Afghanistan: The Reign of Amir Dost Muhammad Khan*, (*1826–1863*), Routledge/Curzon, 1998.

Spain, James, *The Way of the Pathans*, Oxford University Press, Oxford, 1975.

Raverty, H. G., *Notes on Afghanistan and Balochistan*, 2 vols., 1881, reprint Nisa Traders, Quetta, 1982.

Warburton, Robert, *My Eighteen Years in the Khyber*, London, 1900.

**Numerous valuable works in Pashto, Urdu, and Persian may also be consulted. A brief reference includes:**

Bahadur Shah Zafar Kaka Khel, *Pukhtana Da Tarikh Pa Ranaha Key* (Pakhtuns in the Light of History), (Pashto).

Khattak, Afzal Khan, *Tarikh-i-Murassa*, University Book Agency, Peshawar, 1984.

Khan, Roshan, *Pakhtun Origins and History*, (Urdu), Karachi, 1980.

Shah, Pir Mu'azzam, *Tarikh-i-Hafiz Rahmat Khani*, Pashto Academy, (Pashto, Persian), Peshawar, 1987.

Yusufi, Allah Bakhsh, *Yusufzai Pathan*. Sharif Arta Press, (Urdu), Karachi, 1973.

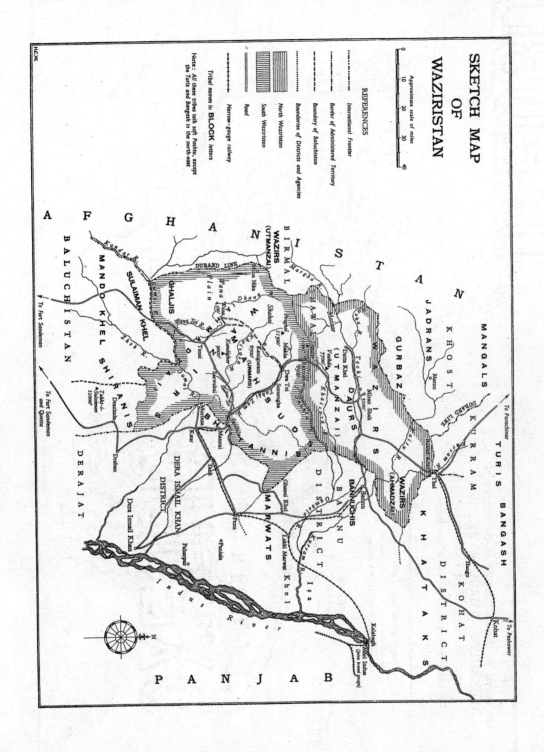

SKETCH MAP
OF
WAZIRISTAN

Approximate scale of miles
0 10 20 30 40

REFERENCES

International Frontier
Border of Administered Territory
Boundary of Baluchistan
Boundaries of Districts and Agencies
North Waziristan
South Waziristan
Road
Narrow-gauge railway

Tribal names in BLOCK letters

Note: All these tribes talk soft Pashtu, except
the Turis and Bangash in the north-east

H.C.W.

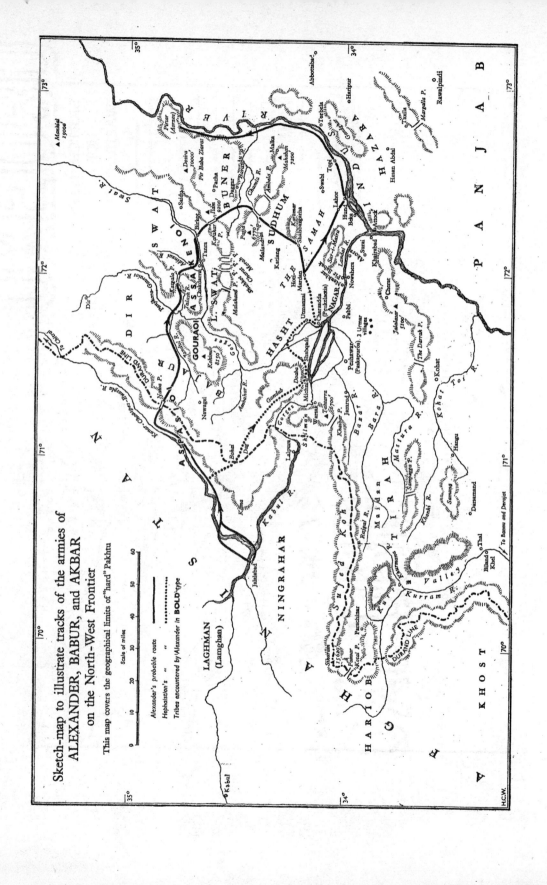

Sketch-map to illustrate tracks of the armies of
ALEXANDER, BABUR, and AKBAR
on the North-West Frontier

This map covers the geographical limits of "hard" Pakhtu

Scale of miles

Alexander's probable route
Hephaistion's       "       "
Tribes encountered by Alexander in **BOLD** type

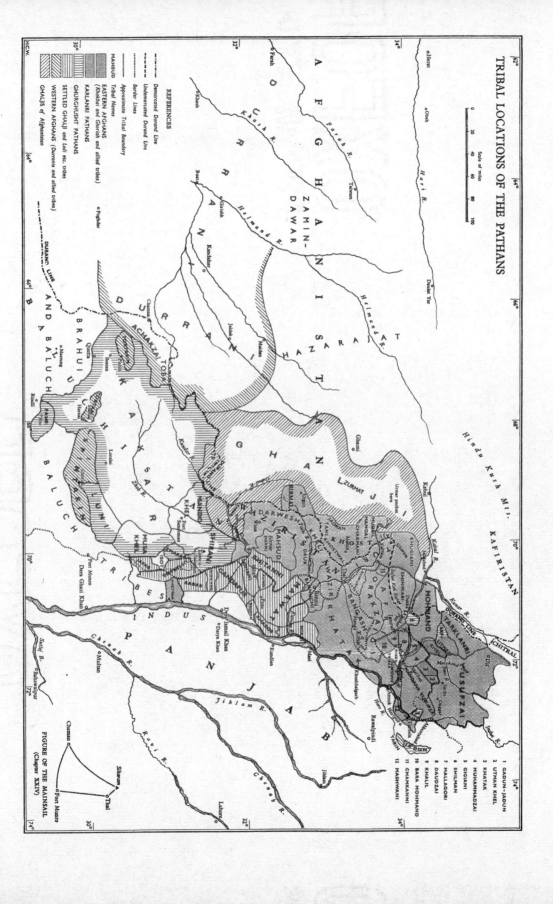

# TRIBAL LOCATIONS OF THE PATHANS

Scale of miles

0  20  40  60  80  100

## REFERENCES

| | |
|---|---|
| Demarcated Durand Line | |
| Undemarcated Durand Line | |
| Border Lines | |
| Approximate Tribal Boundary | |
| *Tribal Names* | MAHSUD |
| EASTERN AFGHANS (Khakbar and Ghorbih and allied tribes) | |
| KARLANRI PATHANS | |
| GHURGHUSHT PATHANS | |
| SETTLED GHALJI and Lodi etc. tribes | |
| WESTERN AFGHANS (Durranis and allied tribes) | |
| GHALJIS of Afghanistan | |

H.C.W.

1  GADUN-JADUN
2  UTHAN KHEL
3  KHATAK
4  HUNAHHADZAI
5  GIGIANI
6  MALLAGORI
7  SHILMAN
8  DAUDZAI
9  KHALIL
10  BARA MOHMAND
11  CHAMKANNI
12  MASHWANI

FIGURE OF THE MAINSAIL
(Chapter XXIV)

Chaman
Fort Munro
Sikaram
Thal

# PART ONE

# NOTES ON WANA

BY

## F.W. Johnston

*(Recorded in 1903)*

# 1

# The Wana Plain

As regards the remote history of Wana, we have no definite information. Doubtless, being a broad, fertile and well irrigated plain, it was much used as a halting place and line of communication by the various tribes who in past times have swept down into Hindustan. But on this point the local history is silent. The first record we have is of occupation by the Marwat* tribe, the majority of the tribe living in the hills now called Marwatis, and the section inhabiting the Wana plain. These, however, were soon dispossessed by the Nasirs, and the history of the last few generations is of the struggle between the Powindas and the Darwesh Khel Wazirs.

2. The Powindas are divided into Nasirs, Suleman Khels, Kharotis, Dotannis, Mian Khels, and miscellaneous tribes, including the Kundis, Mianis, etc. The first two sections are the most numerous and powerful. As the customs and habits of the tribe are so well-known, it would be superfluous to give any further account here, but anything connected with this Agency will be dealt with later in the chapter on the Powinda Migration.

3. The Wazirs, or to be more accurate the Darwesh Khel, claim descent from one Musa,† called Darwesh on account of his pious habits, and it is to the latter's brother that we are said to have been indebted for the Mahsuds. The various ramifications of the Darwesh Khel tribe are shown in the appendix and will be dealt with later, but it is only with one small section enjoying $1/16$th share in the whole tribe, the Bomi, or perhaps Bahami, Khels, that we have to do at present. This section is divided into three tribes,—the Zalli Khel, the Taji Khels, and the Gangi Khels. The first is the largest, and the first two are by far the most important. These seem to have been forced out of Birmal and to have been leading a pastoral life in the hills round the Wana plain, whence again the growing number of the Mahsuds was tending to force them forward.

4. The situation was then, the Powindas occupying the Wana plain, and the Bomi Khels in the hills surrounding being pressed forward by other Wazirs coming up behind.

---

*There are still traces of cultivation on the far side of the Marwatis in Zindswar ascribed by the Wazirs to the Marwats.—J. B. B.

†His ziarat is in Zindawar, and just inside our border.—J. B. B.

5. The affairs at this point have been so clearly stated in a note by the late Mr A.J. Grant that I cannot do better than give the history in his words:-

Several generations ago the influence of the Nasir Powinda tribe was predominant in Wana, and from Wana all along the Toi down to Toi Khulla, its junction with the Gomal. In the centre of Wana near the Dotanni 'Starkot' (or tribal fort) is still visible among the fields a raised line of ground showing the outlines of what is said to have been once a very large Nasir fort. The Dotannis then began gradually to acquire influence in the same neighbourhood and to share with the Nasirs the interests in these tracts. Thus most of Wana passed into the hands of the Dotannis, the Nasirs only retaining their control over isolated portions, such as the 'upper kach' lands on the left high bank of the Toi nearly opposite the Shin Warsak point, thc Ghilzaiwala land at the foot of the Ghilzai Peak, and the Speshta land below Ghilzai on the left bank of the river. The Toi from Ghzha-pazha to Sarizao remained entirely with the Nasirs, while the Dotannis occupied nearly the whole tract from Sarizao to Toi Khulla, with the exception of certain isolated 'kaches', such as Larwam or Dargaddai, which remained in the hands of the Nasirs. While things were in this state about four generations ago the Nasirs made a large and successful raid on the Wazir flocks at a place called Tumanwam, near the head of the Urmana Nullah at the foot of Girni Sar. This raid provoked much bitterness and gradually spread into a wide feud between the two tribes, which was carried on with so much energy and determination by the Wazirs that the Nasirs were obliged to abandon their possessions in the Wana and Toi tracts. Speaking broadly, these possessions appear to have passed into the hands of the Wazirs without any successful protest or claim being made by the Dotannis to obtain them. This occupation of the Wazirs by conquest is, for instance, quite unchallenged by the Dotannis in the case of the 'upper kach' and Speshta lands in Wana and the kaches on the Toi between Ghzha-pazha and Sarizao. On the other hand, the conflict of claims between the Wazirs and Dotannis as to certain of the 'Nasir' kaches in the Lower Toi is due to the fact that the Wazirs here claim the same occupation by conquest, while the Dotannis maintain that the old Nasir rights were absorbed by themselves as pre-emptors or occupiers of the neighbouring lands. Thus in the case of the Dargaddai Kach the Dotannis maintain that when the Nasirs had to leave, they (the Dotannis) bought up their interest; and in Larwam a Nasir claimant asserts that he has continuously retained possession, living as a 'hamsaya' of the Dotannis, while the Wazirs in both cases claim the usual occupation by conquest. In the lowest part of the Toi from Spelipan to Toi Khula the old Nasir claims seem never to have been absorbed by either the Dotannis or Wazirs, probably because this tract lies on the main Khajuri route, and was traversed each spring and autumn by huge Powindkirris, which rendered hopeless any attempt at Cultivation. By the Settlement of 1895 these tracts fell to the Dotannis, though apparently under the terms of Punjab Government letter No. 823, dated 16 July 1895, the Nasir claims here may still be considered to be reserved. Turning from these old times to more recent history we find that 40 years ago the only fort standing in Wana was the Dotanni 'Starkot'. The Wazirs grazed freely in Wana and the neighbourhood and cultivated to a small extent for the Dotannis, paying them owner's rights, which they probably reduced in amount as their own influence became stronger. The Zalli Khels were at this time associated with the Hassan Khel section of the Dotannis and the Taji Khels with the Umar Khel section, who were the more powerful. Each of these sections handed over their rights (or perhaps only the cultivating rights) in the upper Ghwaekhwa land to the Wazir sections with which they were associated. The Taji Khels then approached the Zalli Khels with the proposition that they should unite to construct a big watercourse to carry the Toi water on to this land. The Zalli Khels not agreeing, the Taji Khels alone carried out the work and enjoyed their share of the cultivation for a year or two, after which the Zalli Khels claimed their share in the water which the Taji Khels naturally refused to give, and thus a dispute arose between the two sections. About this time, some 35 years ago, Karim Khan, father of the Malik Gulan, Sheikh Bazid Khel, who was then the most powerful Zalli Khel Malik, built the Zalli Khel 'Starkot' on the Wana 'Dag' land. The Dotannis would not allow the Wazirs thus to establish a permanent footing for themselves in the valley, and, calling in the assistance of the Suleman Khels, made efforts to dislodge the Zalli Khels and destroy their fort. These attempts were continued unsuccessfully during two or three years until the Powindas determined to raise a final powerful combination in the following autumn to make sure of success. The Zalli Khels now approached the Taji Khels in 'Nanawati' to invoke their assistance, but the latter made the abandonment of the Zalli Khel unjust claims to Ghwaekhwa a condition of their help, and this the Zalli Khels refused. The Taji Khels thereupon went off to Urgun, and agreed to assist the Dotannis and Suleman Khels in their impending attack. On the other hand, the Kharotis, who were at feud with the Suleman Khels over a murder case, threw in their lot with the Zalli Khels. In the fighting which occurred the next autumn with the Suleman Khels, Dotannis and Taji Khels were thus arrayed on one side against the Zalli Khels and Kharotis. The Taji Khels, in view of their hostility to the Zalli Khels, made in consideration of their assistance to the Dotannis, thought it advisable and were allowed to build a tribal (Panj guna) kot for themselves, which is still standing and occupied, not far from the ruined Dotanni 'Starkot'. The autumn campaign began with a fight in the upper end of the Wana Valley, in which the Zalli Khels' allies were caught between two fires, being attacked by the Suleman Khels coming down from the mouth of the Dhana and the Taji Khels and Dotannis, who took position on the detached Dzha Ghundi rocks north of the Shin Warsak Spur. The Zalli Khel allies were defeated, fled and took refuge in their tribal kot. The other side followed up their victory by driving off about 3,000 head of Zalli Khel cattle, which they came up with below the Ghzha-pazha point. After this began a long siege of the Zalli Khel tribal kot, in which the assailants suffered the more severe losses, but were in the end successful in compelling the garrison to submission. The Zalli Khel allies were allowed to march out of the fort with their effects, and its walls were then razed to the ground. The Zalli Khels made it a condition of their surrender that the Taji Khels should, like themselves, be forbidden to establish a permanent footing in Wana. The fall of this fort occurred about 32 or 33 years ago.

In the following year the Zalli Khels determined to avenge the raiding of their 3,000 cattle, and, having summoned to their assistance a Mahsud lashkar from Kaniguram, they carried off a large number of the Dotanni flocks. The leader in these reprisals was Bokai, the father of Muhammad Afzal Khan, and the then leading Malik of the Utman Khels. Not long afterwards he was invited by the Dotannis to their 'Starkot' and treacherously murdered by them. To avenge his death the Zalli Khels sent for another Mahsud lashkar and destroyed the Dotanni 'Starkot', its occupants fleeing for their lives to Tattai on the Toi. From this time onwards the Wazirs began gradually, but surely, to usurp the leading position previously occupied by the Dotannis in Wana. The Dotannis lived mostly at Tattai and on the Toi. Those who remained in Wana were given shelter for two or three years in the Taji Khel tribal fort, after which they built up and occupied their Ghwaekhwa fort, the walls of which had been already built, but stood empty. As the Taji Khels did not abandon their tribal fort, the Zalli Khels determined also to make good their footing in Wana, and within a year or two of the fall of the Dotannis' 'Starkot' the Zalli Khel kots of Gulsher and Banocha on the Upper Ghwaekhwa and that of Muhammad on the Toi left bank opposite were built. In establishing themselves thus the Zalli Khels were backed up by the (tacit) protection of Muhammad Akram Khan, Suleman Khel, who pocketed considerable sums of blackmail from them, and this it was which really assured their position. They were harassed nevertheless by the quarrels and jealousies of the Taji Khels, until a few years later they made up their differences about Ghwaekhwa, the Zalli Khels obtaining the half rights they had claimed. From this time onward different Taji

Khel and Zalli Khel kots sprang up over the Wana plain, and the disintegration of the Dotanni control set in rapidly. This was probably between 20 and 25 years ago. We learn from the evidence of the Dotannis themselves in many of their Wana claims, notably that to the Lower Ghwaekhwa land, how their grasp gradually relaxed. In the winter, when their grazing kirris were occupying the Spin and Toi tracts, they were able to hold their own, but each autumn, when they came back from their summer quarters in Afghanistan, they would find that the Wazirs had made some more encroachments on their lands. Thus at a period from 15 to 20 years ago most of their ownership rights in Wana passed out of their hands into those of the Wazirs nominally on mortgages. It is evident, however, both from the nominal amount of the mortgages and from the admissions of many of the Dotannis that the Wazirs would not allow them to redeem, that the rights of the Wazirs were really held adversely. But the cultivation up to the period of four or five years before our coming to Wana still remained to a great extent in the hands of the original Dotanni owners, or, in the case of the Dotanni owners who belonged to the Powinda classes, in the hands of the original Dotanni cultivators. The alienation of the Dotanni lands in Wana by nominal mortgages rather than by sales appear to have been due to two causes,— firstly, that it to some extent saved the pride of the Dotanni owners; and, secondly, that it left an opening for the original owners in case the Dotanni influence should once again become predominant in Wana to claim their own lands under the rules of 'Shariat'. The Dotanni position on the Toi, and especially in the upper part near Tattai, was also all this time not free from Wazir intervention. In the winter, when their grazing kirris were present, the Dotannis could stand on their own bottom, but through the summer those who remained behind were too feeble to protect themselves against Mahsud raids, and used to invoke the assistance of the powerful Zalli Khel Maliks, such as Karim Khan, Bokai, etc., who would send influential men of their sections to remain with them in the Toi as guests and protectors. Thus the Zalli Khels obtained a footing in the Dotanni Toi also, partly as genuine mortgagees, and partly in virtue of the protection they afforded the Dotannis in the summer.

6. This brings the history of the Dotannis and Wazirs in Wana down to the period almost immediately preceding our arrival and occupation. In anticipation of our coming the Wazirs felt themselves strong enough to put their own position in Wana on a more definite basis and stultify all Dotanni claims. The relation between the two tribes up to the very time of our coming had been in all matters, including those connected with cultivated land, entirely tribal and not at all individual. Undoubtedly all alienations of Dotanni land to Wazirs by the individual owners had been carried out with the tribal consent and sanction, either express or by the

waiving of their pre-emption rights. Even up to late years each autumn when the Dotanni kirris came down in force into Wana, the tribe had been able to recover from the Wazirs certain quantities of grain on account of lands to which the Dotannis still laid claims, but the cultivation of which had long ago passed into the hands of the Wazirs, more often by implied than by expressed agreement. These sums were extracted from the Wazirs by tribal pressure, by the effect of the united tribal strength of the Dotanni kirris. Thus in the autumn of 1892 the Dotannis assert that one of them, Lagure, had got from the Zalli Khels Rs. 70 in cash or kind on account of his somewhat vague claim to the old Mehr Khan karez which had once watered the 'Dag' land on which Zorawar had since built his kot without the Dotanni consent. In the autumn of 1893, however, a similar claim on the part of Lagure was met by the Zalli Khels with a direct refusal. The Dotannis thereupon made an unsuccessful attempt to carry off some Zalli Khel cattle, while a retaliatory raid by the Wazirs on the Dotanni flocks was successful. The quarrel between the two tribes now became acute. Muhmammad Akram Khan and other Suleman Khel Maliks came up to Wana from Zarmelan to try and mediate, but were unsuccessful. The Dotannis were hemmed in their Ghwaekhwa Kot, and the Wazirs were encouraged to press them hard with the idea of establishing their sole possession in Wana before we came to occupy it. Under these circumstances the Dotannis could not hold out and fled to Tattai, and the Wazirs then destroyed the Ghwaekhwa kot. The Dotannis could not sit still under this outrage at so critical a point in Wana history, and in the course of the cold weather they made arrangements with the other Powinda sections to make a combined 'tora' on Wana on their way up to Afghanistan in the spring of 1894. The Wazirs became much alarmed and came into Tank imploring our aid in effecting some compromise with the Dotannis. After much consultation an agreement was come to in Tank between the parties whereby the Wazirs were to pay Rs. 500 and 500 sheep to the Dotannis in compensation for the damages recently inflicted on them, the Dotannis were to be allowed to rebuild the Ghwaekhwa kot, and the disputed claims to landed rights between the two tribes were to be adjudicated by 'Shariat'. The Dotannis thereupon dispersed the combined 'tora' they had arranged, and in the spring came up to Wana to obtain the consummation of the agreement. The Wazirs began slowly making over to them the money and sheep which had been assessed to them in compensation, but when only part had been paid a serious Mahsud raid under Jaggar, Abdur Rahman Khel, was made on the Dotannis in Tattai, several of them were killed, and nearly all their plough cattle carried off. The Dotannis were then obliged to abandon for that year the cultivation of the Toi, which previously they had practically always carried out for themselves, and the Toi Dotannis joined their other kirris, who broke off negotiations with the Wazirs and left at once for Afghanistan. They had good reason for believing that the Mahsud raid on Tattai had been organized by the Wana Ahmadzais, and they determined that such a flagrant breach of faith should be signally punished. For the autumn of 1894, therefore, they, with much trouble and expense, made arrangements for a very strong combined 'tora' of all the Powinda sections to ravage Wana and the Mahsud country. This 'tora' was stopped authoritatively by us before our occupation of Wana, and we promised to see that the Dotannis obtained their just rights. If we had not taken action there is no doubt that Wana and the Mahsud country would both have suffered very severely; many of the Wana kots would have been destroyed and all the standing crops would have been laid waste. Our occupation of Wana in fact was timed exactly to suit the Wazirs and to save them from the just vengeance of the Powindas for their faithlessness.'

6. I may add to Mr Grant's note that he made such a satisfactory settlement of the various claims that it has never from that day to this been questioned. The result is that except for one village and the surrounding lands known as Kot Dotanni, the whole of Wana is in the hands of various sections of the Darwesh Khels. Lower down the Toi, from Tattai to Toi Khulla, the Dotannis have still a considerable settlement, but, except for these and the *quasi*-settlement of Zarmelan, the occupation of the Powindas is entirely removed from the Agency.

7. The Wazirs now hold undisputed possession practically of the whole, but there can be no doubt that had not occupation of the country come in 1894, it would not have been long before the same procedure would have been enacted, the Mahsuds taking the place of the Wazirs, and the latter sinking into that of the Powindas.

# 2

# The Wana Ahmadzais and their Lands

8. The Darwesh Khels, as already stated, claim descent from the religious Musa. The practical man is not much concerned with their origin, and still less with their ultimate destination, as that is a point which admits of no doubt.

9. They themselves say that they came from Afghanistan in the neighbourhood of Birmal, and the fact is quite possible. The tribe is not one of very great antiquity. Following out the internal distribution of the tribe, which follows strictly the principles of heredity, the sub-section known as the Karmaz Khels is in the ninth generation from Musa. Up to this Karmaz Samandar, one of the chief Maliks, can trace his descent, name for name, making him his ancestor in the seventh generation. This makes fifteen generations in all from Musa to Samandar, who is a man of about 30. In the same way Mani Khan has traced to me his descent from Sperkai, and the two results practically tally. One might roughly then on this assumption date the original founder of the tribe from 400 years back, but this is hardly justified.

10. The Darwesh Khels are sometimes known as 'Star,' or great, Wazirs in contradiction to the Mahsuds, but as the latter never use the name of Wazir in referring to themselves, it will be sufficient to adopt the common parlance and use the word Wazir only for Darwesh Khels.

11. The Wazirs divide into two main sections the Utmanzai and Ahmadzai*. The former have no dealings here, but as the Wana people, though only a small section of the Ahmadzais, have so intermixed their politics with the whole tribe, it will be more convenient to deal with the

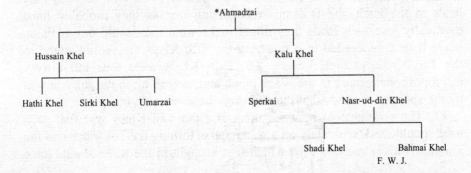

whole of the Ahmadzais. The latter are divided again into the Sain, probably Hussain Khels and Kalu Khels. Among the Hussain Khels by far the largest and most powerful clan is that of the Hathi Khels under Khair Muhammad. The Sirki Khels of Wana also belong to the Hussain Khels, but they are so small in number that their influence is practically *nil*, and they follow their stronger neighbours. Among the Kalu Khels half are the Sperkais, Mani Khan's clan, and half the Shadi and Bomi Khels, who hold Shakai and Wana respectively.

12. Between Mani Khan and Khair Muhammad there is no love lost, and even in his own tribe Mani Khan is not free from the troubling of Jalandhar Shah, the son of his elder brother. The Bomi Khels and Shadi Khels by ties of blood and kin follow the Kalu Khels, and accept Mani Khan's leadership implicity.

13. The tribes in the Wana plain are the Sirki Khels, the Khojal Khels, and the Bomi Khels, consisting of the Zalli Khels, Taji Khels, and Gangi Khels. The last, the Bomi Khels, are practically entirely in Wana. Of the Khojal Khels a portion, and of the Sirki Khels only a few.

14. The Wana plain itself is a large alluvial plain, surrounded entirely by hills, and receiving the water from the two large algads of the Bahmai and Dhana. Along its western and southern sides flows the Toi emerging from the plain at the south-east corner.

15. The lands in and connected with this plain may be roughly divided as follows: The kach lands on the Toi, the Dag or higher plain land lying from the left bank of the Toi to Wicha Khwara in the Inzar Narai direction, and the lands by Tattai and Spin, the latter of which is a plain like Wana on a smaller scale.

16. Of this land the Dhana is in possession of the Gangi Khels. Nearly the whole of the rich kach land on the Toi belongs to the Taji Khels; the Zilli Khels have Spin, while the Dag lands are divided between the Zilli Khels and Taji and Gangi and Khojal Khels. It seems anomalous that while the Zilli Khels did all the fighting for Wana, the Taji Khels should have been able to take possession of the best land. As stated by Mr Grant, the Taji Khels joined the Powindas against the Zilli Khels, and during the cessation of hostilities the Taji Khels were able to acquire on mortgage the lands in the kach, the Dotannis recognizing that as they probably must eventually lose their lands they might make what they could out of them, while if they succeeded in conquering the Zilli Khels they could attend to the Taji Khels at their leisure. The Zilli Khels were thus left a very disproportionate share in the Wana plain, and, according to the story, it was by the shortest of heads that they secured the ownership of Spin.

17. The arrangement between them and the Taji Khels was that each tribe should work separately on a watercourse turning the Toi water into the Zaranni Nullah, and that tribe which first brought in the water should have

sole possession of Spin. The distance is about a mile, and day and night the work carried on by every man, woman or child went on incessantly. Finally, when the Taji Khels had only 20 yards of watercourse to complete, they* heard the water pour into the nullah from the Zilli Khel wial. From that day they have never obtained an inch in Spin.

18. As regards these individual lands. The kach lands starting from Shin Warsak have practically all been mapped and a kishtwar register prepared. On the right bank of the Toi are the Ghoikho lands and Painda Khan Karez. To these the same remark applies. It is on this kach land that nearly all the villages and towers are situated. The land is very rich, well watered, and contains many trees. Should it ever be desired to coerce the Wana people, an explosive party moving along the Toi could do lakhs of damage.

19. The Dag lands have been divided among the Taji Khels, Zilli Khels, Gangi Khels and Khojal Khels. The last received their share on account of assisting the Zilli Khels in their struggle with the Dotannis. The boundaries have been clearly fixed. The land to the south goes to the Taji Khels, the larger portion in the middle to the Zilli Khels, the portion west of Shin Warsak to the Gangi Khels, and the portion to the north up to Inzar Narai to the Khojal Khels.

20. There is a small piece of cultivation west of Inzar Narai, which was claimed by all these clans, but by unanimous agreement in 1902 this was handed over to the Moghal Khels, to whom I gave the old levy post to live in on† condition that it should be considered outside the protectorate, and that they should make their own arrangements for its protection. Further down the Toi, where it leaves the Wana plain, the land belongs to a miscellaneous collection. Mahsuds, Shakiwals and Hathi Khels all own portions. Below this again the land belongs to the Zilli Khels. The latter have just come to an agreement that this land is not to be watered‡ from the Toi, all the water of which is to go to Spin, except that the faqir at the ziarat is to receive a moderate amount.

21. This dag§ land is mostly alluvial plain covered into scrub. When irrigated it gives excellent crops. The portions of it are mostly known by the names of various karezes which used to, and some of which do now, supply water to it. It is also watered by two wials known as the Shui and Kareza.

22. By the present Wana Fort is an excellent spring which provides abundance of water. This fort was built on the site of a Khojal Khel village, and the Khojal Khels are to this day sore on the subject of compensation,

---

*They got very near the Zaranni, but came to a great pit below it. If they had had sense, they might have made a lake.—F. W. J.

†They agreed to this, but thought I was going to be weak enough really to protect it. Now that I have put it outside, they refuse to hold it. I have consequently ordered it to be knocked down.—F. W. J.

‡Yes, and they fight about this all day now.—F. W. J.

§Names of Karez are—Ashraf, Makhar, Mahr Khan, Akhund, Landa by Tahsil, Malik.—F. W. J.

which they allege was far too small, as in fact it was. From the line drawn east and west of the fort the land to the west is all stony raghza.

23. Spin* itself belongs to the Zilli Khels alone. They have lately partitioned it, and been constantly troubling over the interpretation and completion of this petition. The matter has been settled, but they will probably try to revive it.

24. Following the Toi we have the land[†] at Tattai, part of which have been given to the Darwesh Khels, the Dotannis, however, retaining the right to cultivate, and the Chinikho lands higher up on a branch stream. The major portion belongs to Dotannis. The Wazirs are always trying to do the Dotannis out of their cultivating rights, and have to be watched.

25. To the north is the Dhana, consisting of a narrow valley well watered, and laid out in plateaus of excellent soil. To the east of that again is Shakai at a considerably greater elevation, consisting of flattish land well watered, and opening into the Khaisara by Torwam. At the top of the Dhana is beautiful country, and all round by the Marwatis are possibilities of hill stations better than any I have ever seen.

26. Of the tribes in Wana the largest and most important are the Zilli Khels. Like all the other tribes, these are to be found in any numbers in Wana in the spring and autumn only, when they are chiefly in Spin. In summer they go to the hills, and in winter some go to Kashmir Kar and others to the winter mela in Narshish near Murtaza. One of their sections, the Kaka Khel, live almost entirely by grazing, while the Utman Khels are also very largely indebted to their cattle for their livelihood.

27. The Taji Khel go very considerably to Birmal and Kohat. They are always getting mixed up with the Khalifa of Murgha, who tried at one time to exercise a co-ordinate jurisdiction in Wana affairs. They very largely take up Commissariat contracts, and have the largest number of bad characters.

28. The Gangi Khel are a comparatively small and very wild section, living mostly in the Dhana. They come little into Wana, but are quiet enough.

29. The Khojal Khels have largely left Wana since their land was taken for the fort. They live round and about the village of Dabkot near the fort.

30. The Sirki Khels have land in Kazhapunga above Shin Warsak, and also in the Ghoikho. Their best[‡] land in Talbana Kach was taken-rather unnecessarily for the fort, and they have not yet taken compensation.

---

*See note on this in appendix.—F. W. J.

[†]It is a case of six and a half dozen. I have ordered that Wazirs may not build kots Tattai way, but that if the Dotannis continue their habits of molesting cultivators and stealing Wazir cattle, I will let the Wazir build as many kots as they like. Also if the Dotannis bring a lashkar into Wana, they will be flung out of Tattai altogether. If the Dotannis kill Dawe, they will get into trouble.—F. W. J.

[‡]This is all settled now.—F. W. J.

31. There is a great dispute about Kazhapunga. At the desire of all the Wazirs I put that outside the protectorate, but ordered that it was to be considered protected in so far as any unlawful violence was given to the Sirki Khels, and that if any other tribe had a suit, it was to be settled by me by Shariat.

32. There is a dispute also about Manji Oba, but I am going to leave them to fight this out among themselves.

# 3

# The Wana Ahmadzais Particularly

33. In writing this chapter, which can be of no interest to any one except my successor, it appears to me unnecessary to enter any remarks as to the merits or failings of the various Maliks, since that is a matter on which even among men on the spot at the same time the greatest diversity of opinion can prevail. Even as one does not attempt to shave with a tooth brush, or brush his teeth with a razor, so all Maliks can do excellent work if properly applied, while to put them all in the same category, and treat them all in the same hard-and-fast way, is sure to result in the disfavour of many.

34. It will, I think, be sufficient if I give a description more particularly of the various sections, stating the name of the more important Maliks, and giving particulars of the various feuds and law suits of which it is necessary for the Political Agent to have a clear understanding.

35. As the Political Agent will be perpetually worried by would-be beneficiaries who were done out of their rights during their unavoidable absence from Fort Sandeman, or who lost by going to the Amir, I append a short account of the history of the Wana Maliki.

36. Before the occupation of Wana, when the question of allowances to Darwesh Khels was first mooted, the tribe was called in by Sir R. Sandeman to Fort Sandeman, better known here as Pezi (Appozai). A certain number of the smaller Maliks for reasons of their own did not choose to attend, and indubitably the other representatives of their sections took advantage of their absence to their own profit.

37. Then in 1891-92 the Amir raised the question of his claims to Wana, and a number of the leading Maliks—Gulan, Gulsher, Bannochi, Sher, Band—went up to Kabul and accepted allowances from the Amir. The first three received Rs. 60 each, Sher Rs. 50 and Band Rs. 30. Then came the visit of Sardar Gul Muhammad Khan to Wana, on which it seems unnecessary to dwell here. A large number of the Maliks, however, among whom were Zorawar, Minabat, Samandar, Dawe, Qadir, Topchi, Mirza Gul, Khimar, Amir, refused to accept allowances at the hands of the Amir, and proceeded to Tank. Then came the Durand Agreement, and the wandering Maliks after some discussion were received back into the Government fold. After the Mahsud attack in 1894 a large number of Mahsuds went to Kabul. With them went Faqir and Kasim who had been in receipt of Rs. 30 from

the Amir and Rs. 2 from Government. After a considerable stay in Kabul they found it more convenient to return to Wana. For a long time their Maliki was held in abeyance, but was finally restored.

38. The Zilli* Khels are divided into three main sections,—the Sheikh Bazid, the Kaka, and the Utman Khel.

39. *Sheikh** Bazid Khel.*—This tribe has its summer mela in Nargassi and Khijana Toi, and with all the other sections of the Zilli Khels has joint winter melas at Narshish, Kashmir Kar and Manzai.

*Genealogically the tribe goes:—

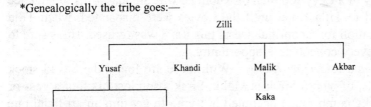

In practice it devides:—

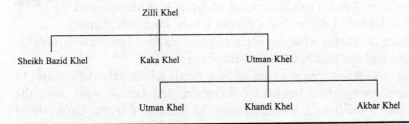

**The Sheikh Bazid Khels genealogically:—

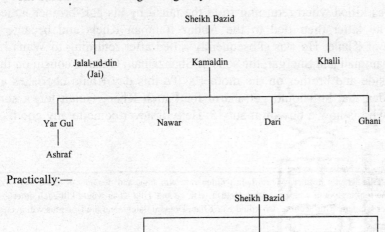

Practically:—

Sheikh Bazid

Ghani and Dari        Jai

Ashraf with Nawar        Yar Gul with Khali

F. W. J.

15

40. For practical purposes it ignores its genealogical tree and divides into three sections, or to be more accurate 2 2/2.

41. *The Jai Khels.*—Maliks Tilla Khan, Aikam (Hakim), Karai's son under the guardianship of Mahmit Khan—Motabirs Ghulam and Ghazo. Ghulam is the brother of Gulsher, deceased, the father of Tilla* Khan and takes a very large share of his work. It is a question whether he should not get a share of his allowance. Gulsher appears to have been a very fine man, and did excellent work for Grant, who allowed him to himself draw without service the pay of a Levy footman of whom he was Silladar. This indulgence was continued to Tilla Khan until the Levies were disbanded, when Tilla Khan's application for a continuance of this Rs. 8 was refused. He is sure to ask for it on every conceivable opportunity.

42. *The Ghani and Dari Khels.*—With these are found the Sayad stock of Dinar Khels, of whom Sirak is Malik. Sirak's son lost his foot a year or two ago, and he is too much occupied in trying to get him an artificial one to have any time to attend to anything else. The Dari Khel Malik is Dawe,[†] who has large interests at Tattai, and is always trying to get his Dotanni cultivators turned out. The Ghani Khel Malik is Raz Muhammad.

43. *The Ashraf Khels,* with the Nawar Khels, take ¹⁄₆th share.

44. There are no Government Maliks in this section. The leading motabar is Gulazan, and the family of Guls belong here.

45. *Yar Gul Khels,* with whom are the Khali Khels, take 1/th share. In this section are the two houses of Bannocha and Gulan, who, with the Gulsher above mentioned, were formerly the leaders of Wana. Gulan owed his position more to his father Karim Khan, who built the large Wazir kot near the tahsil alluded to in Grant's note already quoted. Some years ago Gulan was killed when returning from the tahsil by his half-brother Fatteh Khan. The latter then fled to the Abdur Rahman Khels and became a hamsaya of Khalo. He was subsequently killed after returning to Wana by Ata Muhammad and Shergai, the sons of Shahzaman, Gulan's cousin on the father's side and brother on the mother's. To this day Khalo cherishes an absurd idea that he should get sharm for Fatteh Khan. Gulan left a son, Guldin, who is now a boy of about 15. He will never come to any good.

---

*Lately Tilla Khan's brother. Mehrdil, has fallen out with him, and demands a share. He is an unwholesome looking youth with projecting teeth. I wish he and Tilla Khan would kill each other and make way for Ghulam. This section also killed Nur Khan, Dotanni, lately, and the Dotannis will avenge this.—F. W. J.

Tilla Khan has killed Mehrdil.—J. B. B.

†Dawe is a good man, though he does worry Dotannis, who have lately stolen his horse. I have given Dawe the cultivating rights through Dotannis of Massuzai land formerly cultivated by Lagure. Dawe is also suspected of complicity in Nur Khan's killing. The Dotannis should not be allowed to kill Dawe.— F. W. J.

46. Bannocha is getting old and past his work. At one time he was becoming a Darwesh millionaire. He had one son, Bahawul, a Subadar in the Militia, one son, Maizulla, a Jemadar in the Levies, and another Azmat, a sowar. Now Bahawul has gone and the Levies have gone, and Bannocha is going*. His eldest son, Paio, though a most agreeable young man, does not seem to have much stuff in him.

47. No note on the Yar Gul Khels would be complete without a mention of the veracious Awali, the marvel of Waziristan, a Darwesh Khel whose statements can always be depended upon. He has a special place and a lungi of Rs. 50 which he receives from Political funds on New Year's Day all for himself, and is acknowledged to stand alone. He wanted to build a house near Kot Dotanni, but was told to build it on the other side. He has done so, and his house should be left alone.

48. This finishes the Sheikh Bazid Khels. They are very large numerically, and suffer from being too big for their place. As a consequence in any raid that goes on there is usually to be found an assortment of riffraff Sheikh Bazid Khels.

49. Formerly the badmash element was centered in the family of Guls,—Zar Gul, Mai Gul, Yar Gul. But these have of late reformed, and their reformation has been accelerated by Zar Gul's getting 7 years over a rifle and Mai Gul being put on the security of the whole Zilli Khels, whereupon he made himself a Subadar. They think they have some rights to land in Pipal Kach by Tor Khel, over which they have no more rights than I have, as all the land there belongs to the Dotannis.

50. *Kaka Khels.*—This section have their share in Spin, and what little they have managed to annex in Wana. But they live mostly by grazing, and own large flocks and herds. They have summer melas at Shin, Bahmai, and use Kashmir Kar very largely as a winter mela, where they trouble the Sherannis much.

51. They divide into two main sections,—the Ghulam Khels under Akhund and the Karim Khels under Badshah Khan, the son of Zorawar, Janai and Minabat. Minabat believes that he is the real and only Kaka Khel Malik, and he is certainly no worse than some. Janai is generally out grazing up above or in Kashmir Kar, except when he comes in to try and raise his case with his cousins Khangali, Sharab, &c. These had a great law suit about a piece of land called Ghiljai, and the amount of lying the case produced was something phenomenal. It is now settled, but nobody is pleased. When not stealing cattle from Sheranni territory Janai is losing his own. He is now in security to pay Re. 1 for every sheep lost through want of badragga, and double if he does not report it. The big Malik of this section was up to last year Zorawar. He had a kot east of the tahsil on the

---

*And Azmat has chucked.—F. W. J.

17

Toi adjoining a Gangi Khel kot. There is a piece of land there called Taran belonging to the Gangi Khels about which there had been in the past much hanky panky, and over which Zorawar was trying to do some more. As a result one morning a row took place between the two tribes, and Zorawar walking out to inspect it was stabbed by one Pash, Gangi Khel. Dori, the owner of the kot, Majid, his nephew, the present owner, and Pash, all Gangi Khels, were taken to gaol. Dori died in gaol, Majid was let out, and Pash got a lifer, which was subsequently commuted by the Chief Commissioner to Rs. 1,000 blood-money. The parties were then put on Rs. 3,000 security not to continue the killing. Anyhow when Pash was going down to do his lifer he was taken so bad with dysentery at Kajuri that the doctor there stopped him. After a day or two it was announced that Pash was about to die, his chains were taken off, and he was laid in the hospital and left alone, expected to die in a couple of hours. Instead he jumped off the wall of the Kajuri Post, broke his ankle, and crawled half way to Spin under the Zargar Pel, where he met a man and sent a message by him to a friend in Spin. However, this man had his doubts, so he informed some Kaka Khels, who promptly discovered Pash and cut his throat. They buried him by the Zargar Pel. A few days after, fearing that there would be a search for the body, they exhumed it, cut it into small pieces and threw it into the Gomal. That was then the end of Pash, Dori and Zorawar. The matter leaked out, as everything does, and finally the parties agreed to give the Gangi Khels back their Rs. 1,000 and to cry quits. The heads of parties were Khakim, Gangi Khel, and Stanedar, Zorawar's brother. The Taran case has now been definitely settled. The Kaka Khels have been put in possession of what they have got, and forbidden to acquire any more.

52. Zorawar's place is filled by his second son, Badshah Khan, a boy of about 15, who gives promise of being a fine man.

53. *Utman Khels.*—These with the Khandi Khels take one-third of the Zilli Khels. How they have managed to get on together so far is a marvel, since up to the other day no one ever knew what share the Khandi Khels took, and the present decision appears to have been a matter of pure conjecture. The question only came up lately, when the Zilli Khels started really to cultivate Spin and began by partitioning it. The Khandi Khels said they were a separate section and would go off by themselves. The Utman Khels said they belonged to them and would go with them. After many disputations and arguments and much wasted time it was finally settled that the Khandi Khels should go with the Utman Khels, and that they should have 56 shares out of 320.

54. The Utman Khels, as separate from the Khandi Khels, divide practically into two sections,—the Ada ($^1$/$_3$rd) and the Hassan Beg (Asambik) Khels rds.)

55. The Ada Khel Maliks are Qadir and Saidin who have a slight dispute over land, but at present it is nothing much. Saidin has always preferred the actual service of Government and was in the Levies as his own Bazgir. His speciality is information, and he is known locally as a 'Josis'. He got a loan to build a karez. This should not be recovered.

56. The Hassan Beg Khel Maliks are Sammandar and Wali Shah's son: their sections Kirmaz and Dassi. Samandar is to my mind far and away the decentest man in Wana. He got a severe loss in July 1902, when the Karmaz Khel flocks, owned chiefly by his cousin Muhammad Afzal, were lifted at Narai Oba by Khalo, but full restitution has now been made, and he has had a good many friendly gifts as well. Dali, one of the Khandi Khel Maliks, has married a sister of Khalo's, and there will be trouble some day if it is not watched, as Samandar's one idea in life at present is to kill Khalo and all pertaining to him. Probably if he did kill Dali he would not do much harm, but he would rid the world of an extremely amusing and pleasant scoundrel.

57. The other Khandi Khel Maliks are Muhammad Akbar and Mira Khel. All these get Rs. 2 each. Mira Khel has an idea that his father was the real and only Malik, and that he should be lifted at least to the Rs. 30 grade. He is very well placed where he is.

58. Among the Utman Khels is one Shahdar Khan, Akbar Khel, a well enough man, who has had some trouble with Samandar, and who has brought Samandar into trouble: he needs watching, and should be put on tribal security if he gives any trouble. At the same time the fault is not entirely on his side. The whole case arose out of the prosecution of a blood feud in and out of independent territory by Azmat and Qadir, Moghal Khels, and a few other irresponsibles. The whole thing is done now, but Samandar does not like Shahdar, and is trying* to do him out of a share he claims in Spin.

59. We now come to the second big clan, the Taji Khels. This clan appears to belong to everybody. Its people go to Birmal, and hobnob with the Khalifa there; they go down to Thal and commit murders for Rs. 5 a head; they go down to Bannu and get caught out as Kabul Khels. They belong to Wana, but seem to live everywhere except in Wana. They have seized upon nearly all the best land in Wana, and are always on the prowl

---

*The matter was settled when I went to Spin. Shahdar Khan got his 11 Akbar Khel shares. At the same time he was put on the joint and several security of all the Zilli Khels.

Since then he has kicked over the traces, raided in Afghanistan, killed three Abdur Rahman Khels in the protectorate, and generally made himself a nuisance. We are now out after him.—F. W. J.

I believe he returned again, and is living in quiet with all forgiven.—F. W. J.

trying to do somebody out of his property, real or personal. Their three big sections are the Malli, Masti and Shamshi Khel.

60. *The Malli Khels.*—The Malli Khel is the most prominent, and is honey-combed with feuds, in all of which Topchi plays a leading part. Topchi* is a man of phenomenal height, and has more brains in his head than the whole rest of Wana combined. I will even let him have the Political Agent and staff. His most intimate friend is Rokhan Khan, better known as 'Reshon', and they are a perfect example of the long and the short of it. I show the main divisions as they stand practically, with their Maliks below them, as they all count:-

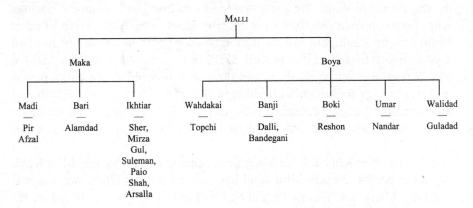

61. The first feud began with Arsalla Khan. Arsalla Khan had a cousin, Momrez, who had a daughter married to the son of Makhal, Topchi's cousin. Arsalla Khan had also a brother, Tarmusa, who claimed that this girl had been given to him. He accordingly abducted her, and for safety became a hamsaya of the Yar Gul Khels. Then he died, and Arsalla Khan married the woman. Topchi raised a lashkar and went to attack him, but he took to his tower, and the assailants had to retire after wounding Arsalla Khan's brother. They, however, set fire to the tower before they went. Paio Shah's chigha came up in time to rescue the inmates of the tower by holding up shawls (takrais) for them to jump into, but the woman jumped through hers and lamed herself for life. Then Topchi began to raise another lashkar, but Arsalla Khan's nephew asked them not to make a business of the matter as he could settle it in a much more peaceable way. He accordingly put poison in the woman's broth, and that was the end of her. However, Khidr Khan, Makhal's son, who was the real villain of the piece, would not rest content. He stole the horses of Arsalla Khan and Paio Shah. The Naib Tahsildar sent for the parties to the tahsil to settle the case. Arsalla Khan did not leave the tahsil till late. On his way home he was seized, and his nose cut off.

---

*Murdered by Dalli, Banji Khel, over Badegani's Ma.—J.B.B.

Rs. 1,000 compensation was awarded and paid, less Rs. 500 as detailed below, and the case seems at an end so far as the Maka and Boya Khels are concerned, but Arsalla Khan is still arguing with Paio Shah about the value of one of those horses; also there is the Rs. 500 fine for firing charged against Paio Shah's party and cut from his nose money. The other culprits have not paid him their share.

62. The real *Pièce de résistance*, the badi of Wana, between Sher and Topachi is only about 3 years old. Topachi has land on the Toi Kach. Gaggar, Pir Afzal and Ahmad have shares there also. A case started on the matter and feeling ran high. A settlement was come to on the spot and carried out. Then in the evening Topchi's people came up quietly and changed the watercourse. Gaggar raised a chigha, and the parties met and words followed. Then Abdur Rahman Topchi's cousin fired twice and wounded two Maka Khels, Stanedar and Mahr Gul. Meanwhile Levies had come up from the tahsil, and the parties were dragged off to the havalat. A settlement was patched up, but neither party paid any attention to it. Just a year ago Abdur Rahman was enticed out of his house and killed by Gaggar in the kach just by Kot Dotanni. Pir Afzal and Gaggar, &c., were tried for the murder, but wrongfully acquitted on oath. Subsequently the parties made a private compromise, Gaggar paying Rs. 1,500 Kabuli. The parties are under heavy security, but still, I fancy, they keep the watches of the night. Go up the kach lands any evening after sunset and stand outside a kot and call for the man of the house. First come the dogs, then the children, then the women, and only after perfect safety has been assured will the master allow his valuable person to be seen.

63. Even in his own Boya Khels Topchi has another little trouble. There is a Mahsud woman, Katti Khel, who married into the Banji Khels. She has a son, Badegani, who, by reason of most of his relatives having been murdered and the blood money being realized (also owing to land), is very rich. Topchi has constituted himself the guardian of this boy, and the Banji Khels are beginning to think that his attentions to the mother are more than those of an older brother. Topchi will get left* one of these days if he doesn't watch it. At present Badegani's money is with me on deposit. On this lad's account Topchi has also run his head against the Dotannis. There is an old Painda Khel blind man, Makhar, a hamsaya of the Dotannis, who owns the dag Painda Khel Karez lands. Topchi claims these for Badegani, and this autumn began forcibly to cultivate them, till he was put in the havalat. This case was settled by me, probably wrongly.

64. So much for Topchi: now for the other side.

65. Sher is as thorough going an old blackguard as you will find west of the Indus. He used perpetually to be hanging about Birmal, till the Khalifa

---

*He has.—J. B. B.

there with rare discrimination took to putting him in gaol. When the British rule was new in Wana, Sher was displeased with a decision as to the Ghoikho lands, and promptly appealed to the Khalifa, who reversed the decision and began to execute his order by laying hands on all parties concerned who happened to be in the neighbourhood. Thereafter, I am told, Sher showed a fine spirit in resisting authority giving any orders on the question, but he is now quieted down marvellously.

66. He has a brother also a Malik, Mirza Gul. Mirza Gul has suffered lately owing to his kirri having been cleaned out by Mahsuds just at the end of the blockade; but he received Rs. 1,000 compensation for it, which was quite ample. He is quite the next best Wazir after Samandar.

67. This leaves Suleman, the only man on the Maka Khel side who has not taken an active part in the fight. He doubtless would have done so had he not constituted himself the Birmal Taji Khel *par excellence*, and is always busy ingratiating himself either with the Khalifa or me. He is a plausible man with a dignified appearance such as one would imagine his namesake had, but is not very trustworthy. However, if you want the latest lies from Birmal to put in an official diary, be sure to send for Suleman.

68. On the Boya Khel side Topchi is pre-eminent, except that the Banji Khels headed by Dalli are beginning to regard him suspiciously.

69. Reshon is only a sarbarah, and if the young man for whom he is officiating comes to his own, Reshon should get the first Maliki going, as he is a very good man. There are no special bad characters in the Malli Khel section, the Maliks having in old days entirely monopolized the privilege.

70. *Masti Khel.*—The Masti Khel divide into five sections, of which one, the Tersam Khel, is practically obsolete. The largest section is the Isa Khel, all of whom live in Wana. To this section belong most of the Government Maliks. The section of whom, however, the Political Agent is likely to hear most is the Khoja Khels who live in the Dhana only, and whose reputation is well kept up by Kashmir and Nizamdin, better known as da Nambali Zamin, though they are really his stepson and nephew.

71. The Isa Khel Maliks Shergul, Zangin and Arsalla Khan do most of the work for the Commissariat in the way of providing wood, goats, &c.

72. They have naturally to take* their bahirs into the unprotected area, but the Mahsuds have been warned not to interfere with them so long as they are on peaceful pursuits, and an attack on a *bonâ fide* wood bahir should be taken up.

---

*Yes, but as soon as the troops move we do not want to protect bahirs. So long as they are willing to bring wood, it seems rather unfair for us to go and cut their wood. When they refuse the Militia will go and cut according to taste.—F. W. J.

73. The Masti Khels had in old times the reputation of being the greatest raiders among the Wana Ahmadzais, and this reputation is still maintained by the Khojal Khels. These have no tower up the Dhana. They live with any one, and under the leadership of Kashmir and Nizamdin maintain a compact little gang of 15 or 20 well armed and thoroughly brave men. To this day they are the only Wana Wazirs for whom the Mahsuds have any respect, and their continued depredations among the Mahsuds continue to make them highly useful as a means of diversion to keep the Mahsuds honestly occupied. In former days they were not so particular to keep their depredations to the unprotected area, and had engaged in various raids on Powindas, for which decrees had been passed against the Wana Ahmadzais. In the spring of 1902 I took up such cases as existed between the Suleman Khels and Ahmadzais, and decided the lot, leaving a balance of some Rs. 1,200 against the Ahmadzais. This was chiefly in Kashmir's name, but I realized from all the Ahmadzais, and set off a decree of Reshon's which was to be realized from Kashmir. He has now paid up practically the whole of this, and need not be worried over it, though Reshon will doubtless come pressing the matter. In the middle of the summer, when Kashmir and Nizamdin were leading an honest life, I gave them Rs. 10 a month each to guard the Dhana against Mahsuds using it as a route to Wana. But as they again misbehaved I cancelled the allowance. Its giving at all was a mistake, as they had made themselves known as bad characters, and to give any allowance to such only makes badmashi a pensionable profession; and as every Wazir or Mahsud is a potential badmash, when one well-known character takes his pension, four successors spring up.

74. Kashmir and Nizamdin's latest, and probably finest, exploit was when they cleared out the Khaisara in September 1902 in return for Khalo's raid on Samandar. They brought away 160 cows and held the whole Khaisara chigha up on the Inzar Narai. They are both very young, probably under 20, and are a merry hearted pair of scoundrels, but rather stupid.

75. The most prominent feud in the Masti Khel section is between these Khoja Khels and the Machi Khels. A Khoja Khel had a quarrel with his own section over a woman, and came as a hamsaya to Kalandar, Machi Khel. The Khoja Khels brought a lashkar on the latter, and Kalandar wounded an old man Nasir, cousin of Dilai, who died after about a year. For many years nothing happened, but in 1902 Kashmir and Nizamdin lay in wait for Kalandar as he left his village in the early morning, and shot him. Kalandar left a brother Bari and a cousin Faqir, a Government Malik, who has been already mentioned as having got left while coquetting with the Amir.

76. However, as Kashmir and Nizamdin were successfully seized by Jacob, I fancy we shall hear little* of them for some time.

---

*Been quiet lately.—J. B. B.

23

77. *Shamshi Khels.*—The Shamshi Khels are not a large section, though they contain some turbulent characters.

78. The Maliks of the three sections are Qasim, Ghazni Khan and Ain-ud-din, Dost Muhammad and Miraband. Dost Muhammad has a quarrel with his cousins, who will probably succeed in ending his existence.

79. Ain-ud-din and Ghazni Khan do Commissariat contract work very considerably. Qasim does nothing in particular, and Dost Muhammad* is very often round at Birmal. Ghazni Khan and his two brothers Wali and Juma Khan were a trio of the greatest blackguards one could hope to meet. The two brothers used to give great trouble at Hangu, and amongst other enormities killed an unoffending boy for a reward of Rs. 5. In the spring of 1902 I managed to catch the two brothers, but as at that time so many Mahsud blackguards were being whitewashed, I thought it only fair to give them a chance too. Accordingly the whole Wana Ahmadzais went security jointly and severally for these two. The effect has been excellent, as they have not so far raised a finger, and if they try to, a judicious enforcement of this security will bring about their speedy deaths. Ghazni has been nominally a reformed character for some years. He is now trying to settle down, and he should be given every opportunity to live honestly.

80. *Gangi Khels.*—This clan is practically entirely up the Dhana in unprotected area. Its members carry on their own business up above, and have not attracted any unfavourable notice since I have been at Wana. Of those who live in Wana, I have already given the story of Khakim and Doir's quarrel with Zorawar, Kaka Khel.

81. Another of their Maliks, Jindai, lives with Zangin, Masti Khel. He has certain disputes with Ain-ud-din, Shamshi Khel, over a piece of land called Tattar. The case has been settled. Adil Muhammad has also a house with Makhal, Taji Khel.

82. Among the Bidai Khels Khanak has a murder to wipe off against Chokhai, with whom also Din has a slight dispute. Jindai has had difficulties with the Turi Khels and Bizan Khels.

83. Din is a Malik of Rs. 2, who insists on being a jasus. He occasionally brings some information, but is more generally hanging about. However, he is an institution and is about half mad.

84. One Sultan Faqir is a very decent member of Gangi Khel society. He was once described in a confidential report as a dangerous man, though the only danger that I can see about him is that if he gets much fatter he may burst.

85. There is also Madar, who has a house on the Drenashtar, and Gul Madar, who is an excellent shikari.

---

*Killed by Mahsuds.—J. B. B.

86. *Sirki Khels.*—These do not call for any great remark, as they consist only of a few scattered hamlets,—offshoots of the tribe,—and are practically the families of Khimar Band, Gul Akhmad and Amir.

87. Khimar, Amir and Sarmast live on the kach by the tahsil. Gul Akhmad and Band have a kot in Choikhwa. Certain land at Talbana Kach belonging to Band's party was taken when the Wana Fort was built. The compensation money he always refused to take, and it is still with me. I propose, however, to offer it definitely to him this spring to take or leave. In any case, should the Military vacate Wana, I think this land, which is really too far away from the Fort, might be restored to its original owners. There was a Sirki Khel Mirza, who was at one time acting as a spy for Mahsuds on the prowl after Wazir flocks. He has presently ceased his evil ways, but should he recommence, seven years would do him good.

88. *The Khojal Khels.*—The Wana Khojal Khels contain representatives of each of the five sections, though only a portion of the tribe is in Wana. The others are in the Tochi and the Kohat side. The number of Khojal Khel Maliks is legion, though I am afraid their efficiency is not in proportion to their numbers.

89. In return for helping the Zilli Khels against the Nasirs the Khojal Khels received the northern Dag lands, including the land on which the Fort now stands. In the matter of compensation they were rather badly treated. As the Government of India absolutely refused to reconsider the matter, all references by them to it should be sternly discouraged. However, if any opportunity occurs of giving out land elsewhere, they should be the first to be considered. Moreover, in giving out for cultivation the superfluous lands belonging to the Fort, they should get as much as possible. There is also a piece of land by Talbana Kach originally the property of Khwaja Hussain, for which he has to this day refused the compensation offered. I propose, however, to offer it to him this spring to take or to leave for once and all. The Khojal Khels seem to have always cherished a grudge against the Fort, and are occasionally perpetrating petty robberies of wood or robbing the garden. They generally get caught out, however. The Garden chaukidars were Khojal Khels. They have now been sacked, and we do it ourselves.

90. The most respected of their Maliks was Shahdad, who died a few months ago, leaving a son Khidr Khan. The most influential is Zariband,* who up till lately was not a Malik. One Malik Mamadi sold his Maliki of Rs. 5 to Mach. His nearest relative was Shadaroz, while it was desirable to get Zariband a Maliki. I accordingly divided this Rs. 5 into three shares but Shadaroz refused to take a share, so that the Maliki is now held equally by Zariband and Mach. An occasional reward to Zariband, if he does well, will not be misplaced. The great feud in this section is that among the Babbar

---

*Dead.—J. B. B.

Khels, the Pir and Guli sections. The matter originated long ago in Birmal. Lately most of the parties have been living in the confines of Shakai. The question came to a head again when Bozanir and Sherabaz, the Guli Khels, managed to kill Lahore and Shamsher, and very nearly got Tarakai. Tarakai came into Wana and tried to raise a lashkar there. Having failed in this, he went to the Abdur Rahman Khels, and by depositing his children with them as hostages got Khalu to raise a lashkar, and cleaned out his enemies' flocks, killing three cousins of Sherabaz: the sheep were given to the Mahsuds. I arrested Tarakai and put him before the whole Ahmadzai jirga. They declared that Shakai was unprotected area, so I took no action on that score; but as Tarakai* is a thorough bad character I only let him go on the whole Ahmadzais going jointly and severally responsible for him.

91. A smaller dispute is that between Ghalmai and Kotan.

92. Ghalmai was a Havildar in the Militia and a very fine soldier, but he was dismissed for selling cartridges in conjunction with Badshah Khan, Saidin Utman Khel's son. He is now working as a garden chaukidar. His brother abducted a woman belonging to the other party. The brother died and Ghalmai† married the woman. In autumn 1902 the other party killed the woman. The case was taken up and compensation paid, but the matter will probably go on.

93. *The Shakiwals.*—The Shakiwals are mostly Shadi Khels, though they contain a sprinkling of Sperkas and Hathi Khels.

94. Their Maliks' names are legion and they are in the unfortunate position of being between the devil and the deep sea. In the winter of 1901, when columns entered the Khaisara, Mr Merk ordered the Shakiwals to protect the flank of Badr from these. They naturally did no good as any one might have known, but from this they have argued a claim to the protection of Shakai. However, when Tarakai brought down his Mahsud gang on Shakai, as I have already stated in the note on Khojal Khels, the entire Ahmadzai jirga, including the Shakiwals, all sympathising with Tarakai, were shortsighted enough themselves to declare Shakai out of the protectorate, and the chance was too good to be missed. Accordingly, if they raise the question of our abandoning them in Shakai, it can be answered that it was of their own desire that Shakai was put outside the protectorate.

---

*Bozanir has killed Tarakai and become hamsaya of Gangi Khels.
The Bomi Khels have banished Bozanir, and will be sorry for it.—J. B. B.
Tarakai was the other day killed by Bozanir. His cousin has arrived to take up the blood feud.

| | | | |
|---|---|---|---|
| Sherabaz ... | Tarakai. | Killed.—J. B. B. | |
| Bozanir. | | | |
| Khidr ... | Saudagar | Killed.—J. B. B. | |
| | Azadi | Killed.—J. B. B. | |

†Ghalmai's house was broken into and his Government Enfield stolen. He accuses Kotan. I have warned the Khojal Khels that unless they put a stop to their petty depredation, I shall break all Maliks.—F. W. J.

95. They are a very foolish people the Shakiwals, and not only cannot cut their losses on Badr, but must be always pursuing a pin prick policy against the Mahsuds. They go up and burn a few crops or drive off a few cows. At present only a few of the Mahsuds, especially the Abdur Rahman Khels, are prepared to treat them seriously, but I am afraid the day is coming when the Mahsuds will repeat the Badr history in Shakai, and we shall have the Badr question only on a much larger scale. I do not think it is any use our trying to interfere in the matter. Let them work out their own salvation. The question of placing a post on Jani Mela was raised, but was very properly negatived. Except for the inevitable tora and fighting from Wana that must necessarily ensue, it would not be a bad thing if the Mahsuds got Shakai, as they want room for expansion badly.

96. The late tenants of Badr, the Moghal Khels, have obtained a piece of ground near the golf course, and have got certain water rights from the Khojal Khel channel. I also gave Shahdad some money to make a karez.*

97. The control of the Shakiwals can at present be easily carried on by pressure from Wana. In October 1902 they came out of their shells and took from Powindas property worth over Rs. 10,000, but they restored the whole within a week. They have a lot of ruffians hanging about their hills and have dealings with all sorts of people. They naturally do not raid Wana, and the Daman and the Tochi are too far away for them to reach, so ordinarily they give little trouble, nor are they given to sheltering outlaws. The best thing to do with them is to leave them alone.

98. Of the Shakiwals, there are the Bodin Khels, of whom Mirabat and Shah Nawaz are the best known. Mirabat has lately killed the son of Shahdad, Bizan Khel, on account of the latter's killing his hamsaya. Shah Nawaz had a law suit with a Michi Khel, Khan Sherin, over certain land near Michan Baba. That case was decided, but Mirabat now claims to raise exactly the same case on the ground that he is a co-owner with Shah Nawaz. Don't listen to him. Of the Khunia Khels, Bhittani, Mirwal and Lalo are the best known. Lalo's son, Zangi was long a Havildar at the Narai Oba Post. I have told him I will make him a jasus if he likes. Lalo's youngest son, a mere boy, has lately killed Kalimai, the best of the Khunia Khels. The Shadakais were originally slaves, who became attached to the Bomi Khels, but they have long lived in Shakai, and are now attached to the Shadi Khels, with whom they can now be more properly reckoned. Rahman is their best known motabir. They are a wild lot, and occasionally hired out as assassins. Of the Bizan Khels the majority are in Bannu. The Shakiwal Bizan Khels are led by Shahdad, who is an absolute fool. There remains of the Shadi Khels the Painda Khels, who are poorly represented, and a few Khojal Khels. There is a considerable section of Sperkais, and Shakai is frequently

---

*Which he has not done.—J. B. B.

visited by Mani Khan's sons generally with a view to making trouble. A few Hathi Khels under Badu complete a highly unsatisfactory assortment. These Shakiwals seem bent on compassing their own destruction. Knowing, as they must, that the Mahsuds would be only too glad to acquire Shakai, not only do they not leave the Mahsuds alone, but each section must be always inviting in Mahsuds to help them to raid each other.

# 4

# Of Wana Generally

99. The constitution of the Wana Darwesh Khels is Maliki pure and simple without any service allowance. Up to September 1902 Levies existed, but so little was the service appreciated that a Silladar had to add his two rupees to the eight given by Government to induce a footman to serve. The same difficulty was found in getting recruits for the Militia. Originally Kalla Khan, brother of Tilla Khan, Jai Khel, was tried as Subadar, but he failed to bring recruits. Then Bahawul, son of Bannochi, Sheikh Bazid Khel, was tried for a year. He was a most excellent boy, but stupid, lazy and unconscientious, and was finally turned out. Kashmir, Masti Khel, was offered a Jemadari, but he refused. Lately Mai Gul, one of the family of Guls mentioned among the Sheikh Bazid Khels, enlisted as a Naik, and is bringing in recruits wonderfully. There is now a full company, with Mai Gul as Subadar, and Makami, Bannochi's cousin, Jemadar.

100. If any proof is needed of the prosperity of Wana under British rule, this is ample. Probably in times of tora the Wazirs will talk of injustice and of their having their hands tied in not being allowed to organize raids, but it will be quite sufficient to compare their condition with that of the Mahsuds, whom they will be at that moment holding out as the most fortunate of men.

101. The Maliki system is comparatively successful in a way, not from any inherent excellence in the system or its method of application, but because, if the Wazirs kick, it must be against the pricks. With the Wana Fort within a couple of miles of plain land, of all their rich villages and lands there is no very strong inducement to take up an active policy of antagonism. As a consequence the work in Wana approaches more to Police work than anywhere else in the Agency. With the dismissal of the Levies sanction was accorded to the entertainment of 30 footmen. These are entirely at the disposal of the Naib Tahsildar, and he appoints and dismisses them himself. With the help of these and a few Maliks he is able to make such arrests as he desires, or to recover raided cattle. Were we to stand entirely aside and leave the Maliks to settle the matter as we do the Maliks among the Mahsuds, I do not think the result would be very hopeful, and the same result would happen with a Naib Tahsildar who preferred his office chair to the saddle. The system of law in force in Wana is not very recondite. In civil cases the Shariat is observed, but care should be taken before admitting

any case to the Shariat. By that excellent, but somewhat confiding, code any false suitor who can find two or three perjured witnesses is enabled to possess himself of the lands of others. It was observed when land was just beginning to acquire a value that all sorts of unreasonable claims were being proved, and an insecurity of tenure was manifested all round. I accordingly adopted the system of making a thorough enquiry, whether privately or publicly, into the facts of each case, and throwing out at once bad cases. This procedure may be off-hand, but it is much the justest. In money cases and the like, to save a long array of decrees to be realized, the best—in fact the only—course is to escort the defendant if the case goes against him, from the court-house to the havalat until he pays. If the successful plaintiff desires to make terms, let him do so on the distinct understanding that if the defendant does not abide by his agreement the Court will take no further action of any kind.

102. Criminal cases from murder downwards, except when they concern Government or Government servants, are generally best taken up as torts, with the exception that cases referring to women should never be touched. Wazirs must kill somebody, just as Englishmen must play games, and it has always appeared to me that so long as they confine their attentions to each other they do not harm either Government or Government prestige. In the present state of society it is impossible to check killings, and to call for the rope in each case simply means that the offender quietly slips over the border and becomes a dangerous outlaw, whereas his incarceration until he pays Rs. 360 generally satisfies every one. But in any case it is useless to lay down, not merely hard and fast rules, but any set of principles, and any officer who comes up the valley with such a set had better leave them or himself at Murtaza.

103. So in the question of raids, whether the return of the property is sufficient, whether blood money should be exacted for any persons killed by the raiders, or whether actual imprisonment should be given depends entirely on the circumstances of the case and the state of local feeling.

104. As regards security in the shape of money bonds, I am afraid I must consider it a farce. Though the Wana people are wealthy, their wealth is entirely in kind, and only realizable at a loss. The security which is really good is special individual tribal security for a bad character. I have stated my views on general tribal responsibility and barampta in the chapter on Mahsuds and need not repeat them, but there is no doubt that when a section individually and collectively goes security for a certain person, it sees that that person never moves. Should he do anything, a well selected selection made at once from the various sub-sections will generally bring about the desired effect. Still this special security* should only be used in

---

*I do not think this tribal security has worked, as it has not stopped offences. I am trying rifle deposits.—J. B. B.

exceptional cases. All the Ahmadzais are under such security for Tarakai, Khojal Khel, the Zilli Khels for Yar Gul, and the Taji Khels for Wali Khan and Juma Khan, Kashmir and Nizamdin.

105. It must be remembered, however, that the Wana protected area has been clearly demarcated and is very small. Except for Government servants and *bona fide* wood-cutting parties, no notice of any kind should be taken of anything happening or any case arising outside that area. If the parties disagree, let them fight it out, and any attempt to interfere is only looking for trouble. Some years ago Government directed the Political Agent to attempt to make a settlement in the Badr case. No decision was come to owing to the parties practically telling Government to mind its own business, and had a decree been given, Government had no intention of enforcing that decree. Its prestige suffered accordingly.

106. Unless you are prepared to put a post in the Dhana and enforce your decrees, leave the Dhana and its little quarrels alone so long as they keep them up the Dhana. If two Wana Wizirs like to settle up their disputes in Shakai, and one of them is killed, why worry? It is one Wazir the less.

107. Finally, on the subject of administration I may quote two proverbs,—one that a man cannot be in two places at once; the other that it is foolishness to keep a dog and do one's own barking. The Political Agent's work takes him to Sarwakai and Tank, and if the Naib Tehsildar of Wana cannot be trusted to settle petty cases and to make arrests and report, he will be much better employed looking for bad rupees in the Treasury. The Wazirs are not a secretive people, and if anything is going wrong it will be heard of at once.

108. I have appended a map* showing roughly the land held by the various tribes, but as a matter of fact the Wana people are generally anywhere but in Wana. In the winter they are down at Narsish between Murtaza and Girni, or at Kashmir Kar where Janai is either losing his own sheep or annexing other peoples'; or they are down Thal way worrying the Assistant Commissioner there. In the summer they are up by the Marwatis or Shakai or stretching right down Shawal, or losing sheep to the Mahsuds on the slopes of Janimela. They have at present no burning question among themselves. Spin has been finally partitioned, and a note of the partition duly kept, though it will probably be necessary to go into certain claims of individuals or very small sections. The whole of the Wana lands are being mapped out and a record of rights prepared.

109. All old cases, whether against or by Powindas, were settled by me in 1902, and new ones are taken up as they arise, and settled at once without passing decrees. During the Mahsud blockade the Wana people got a large number of captured cows to compensate for what decrees they had, and at

---

*Not printed.

the end of the blockade all such decrees were wiped out. Accordingly in the spring of 1902 the Wana Wazirs started with a clean slate, and since then there have been no decrees stored up against them, nor are there any decrees realizable in their favour beyond the ordinary give and take of cattle, which are settled as they arise, and which will be found only in my and the Tahsildar's register. As regards the inner development of their land, the karez leading the Toi water into the Zaranni to bring it to Spin should be ready* soon.

110. I gave for this Rs. 3,000 on condition of repayment within 12 years and the furnishing of supplies to the Spin Post. As the Rs. 3,000 came from old compensation money applied to this purpose with the Commissioner's sanction, its recovery or the showing of any accounts is not obligatory, the latter I should say, highly inadvisable. I have also given Samandar certain money to develop his land, and some to the Moghal Khels. This is not to be recovered. Probably in a year or two there will be scope for enormous development in Wana and Spin.

111. When the Military vacate Wana there will probably be more garden space than the Militia care to take up. If so, the question of restoring some of the more distant lands to the Khojal Khels and Sirki Khels might be seriously considered. The printed file on the taking over land for Wana Fort makes interesting reading. Grant was not a weak man whom anyone could put up to representing his case if it were not a good one.

112. The question of maintenance of jirgas at Wana is not a serious one. The Wana Maliks live in the vicinity and receive no kharch, though it is the custom to present them annually, about April, with Rs. 250, Rs. 50 for each section for their services as Munsifs. Awali receives at the same time Rs. 50 for himself. The Shakiwals when they come on jirga receive kharch, but their habit of dropping in and living free for a day or two should be sternly discouraged.

---

*As a matter of fact they have chucked it as hopeless.—F. W. J.
Fortunately.—J. B. B.

# 5

# Relations of Darwesh Khels with Mahsuds

113. The relations of the Darwesh Khel with the Mahsuds have never been cordial, and now they might be described as distinctly strained. In the early nineties the Wazirs raised a lashkar to attack the Mahsuds on account of the latter's continued depredations. The armies met at Barwand near Sarwakai, and the Wazirs were badly defeated. Later the Wazirs brought a larger lashkar into Shakai, but the elders prevailed upon them to effect a peaceable settlement. No great good, however, appears to have come from this settlement, as in 1894, the Wana Wazirs called in the Government to protect them from the Mahsuds. Thereafter, even if relations were not very cordial, here appears to have been a *modus vivendi* between the parties, as the Taji Khel kirris used to encamp unmolested in winter in the Shabur and Khuzhma. However, this peace did not last very long, and the troubling of the Mahsuds after the 1894 expedition began by Ashik and Mira Khel Garrarais lifting 1,600 sheep out of the Khuzhma Nullah. Ashiq in his best days was somewhat of a wag, and when bringing in the raided sheep with his party of twenty well armed men, he was intercepted by the Naib Tahsildar of Sarwakai with six Levies armed with smooth bore muzzle-loaders. Ashiq condoled with that official on his inability to interfere with him, but promised as compensation to send him a full fighting man's dadi or share—a promise which he duly fulfilled. It was shortly after this that Mani Khan raised the question of his tora. The matter will be found fully gone into in the printed Proceedings, but the gist of the matter is this. At that time Badr was a contiguous part of Shakai, and was held by the Moghal Khel Bizan Khels, Adjacent to this was Manochilla, &c., which doubtless at some distant time did belong to the Wazirs, but upon which the Mahsuds had steadily encroached. Over these Mani Khan put forward his claim, and declared his intention to raise an Ahmadzai tora to reconquer them.

114. In the summer of 1900 Government ordered the Political Officer to attempt to bring about a settlement of the Badr question. Accordingly Mani Khan and his friends were sent from Bannu to Sarwakai, and the Mahsuds called in. The question was to be decided by the Shariat, and two Mullas, were appointed arbitrators,—Mani Khan's Qazi for the Wazirs and Salim for the Mahsuds. The matter got hung up at the very beginning by the question as to who was to be plaintiff and who defendant, as that makes all

the difference in the Shariat. No decision of any kind could be arrived at. A third impartial Mulla was called in, but he could do no good. The whole assembly was finally dissolved with no result except that of having made everybody thoroughly dissatisfied with Government and more bitter in the matter. The third Mulla subsequently delivered *exparte* his view of the case in favour of the Darwesh Khels, but as nobody wanted his opinion, or was prepared to take any action of any kind, whatever the finding might have been, the matter did not amount to much.

115. I very much doubt if Mani Khan intended the tora question to be taken seriously; at any rate I am perfectly certain that the majority of the Bannu Ahmadzais, many of whom are not over full of love for Mani, would have absolutely refused to follow him. At any rate, while the subject was in the usual stage of talk, the Government of India stepped in and prohibited a tora. What is exactly a tora and what the Government actually prohibited I have never quite been able to determine, but anyhow, so far as I can see, Mani Khan exactly achieved his object, which was to have a general Ahmadzai grievance and to keep dissatisfaction against Government going. If Government had told Mani Khan clearly that while it would allow no hostile demonstrations, armings or collectings from British territory, but that he and his friends might go up in the usual way to the hills in the summer, and having arrived there, fight to their hearts' content and not return until all fighting was done, I fancy all tora discussions would have died a natural death. But the question dragged and dragged, and I fancy the local officers—I was one of them myself—in their anxiety to see that there was no breach of the order against a tora went rather too much on the other line, and did give the Wazirs to believe that the Mahsuds were being unduly favoured at their expense. Anyhow in September 1901 Mad Amin, Mani Khan's son, arrived in Shakai, practically unaccompanied so far as Bannu was concerned, and with singular fatuity commenced to stir up trouble. A certain number of persons went from Wana, and a quarrel was raised in the vicinity of Badr. The Wazirs seizing their opportunity killed 20 harmless Urmurs. Thereupon the whole of the Mahsuds descended upon them and shut up the garrison, who consisted mainly of Wana Maliks, in one of the Badr towns. Samandar, Utman Khel, had a brisk interchange of shots with Guldad, Abdur Rahman Khel, across a graveyard, in which Samandar was wounded in the shoulder and Guldad in the leg, but otherwise the fighting was of a most contemptible nature. One Mahsud was wounded in the foot, but otherwise nobody was injured. The Mahsuds then cut off the water from the tower, and the Wazirs called a parley. It was finally decided that the Wazirs should march out armed with all the honours of war. The Wazirs accordingly did so, followed by the original inhabitants of Badr, and the Mahsuds have held it from that day to this. Some of the Mahsuds say they hold it as security until the blood money of these Urmurs is paid; others say

they hold it by right of conquest. Anyway they have no intention of abandoning it, and Mani Khan has now something tangible to make a tora about. In the summer of 1902 no action was taken by the Wazirs, but at the present moment they are very seriously debating the question. They are emboldened by the fact that they hope for help from the Tori Khels and probably other Utmanzais, as the Tori Khels have been frequently raided by the gangs of Khalu, Abdur Rahman Khel, and Khan Abdullai. In fact last year Sadda Khan called on the Mahsuds and seriously threatened them with a tora if they continued their course of raiding.

116. If the tora question is seriously raised this year, the only thing I can see to do is to turn all Wana people who want to join it up to the hills, and put them in gaol if they reappear before the fighting is done.

117. Apart from the Badr question there is no doubt that the Wana people suffered considerably during the blockade. In the first place they were practically put under blockade themselves in regard to cloth and grain, while a considerable number of their cattle were lifted. Moreover, there were a large number of decrees previous to the blockade in which nothing was realized. On the other hand they received nearly 400 cows taken from the Mahsuds during the operations, and once or twice helped themselves to Mahsud cattle, while in consideration of their losses I have given them thousands from Political funds, so perhaps, all things considered, they did not come out so badly, and we can now justly call square. Since the blockade there has been a certain small interchange of cattle, but nothing serious occurred except in July 1902, when Khalu's gang descended on 1,600 Karmaz Khel Utman Khel sheep, the property of Samandar's relatives, grazing near Narai Oba. The entire flock was driven off and four men killed. The matter would have been settled at once had it not been interfered with by the return of Mianji, &c., and a little later by Kashmir and Nezamdin, descending on the Khaisara and taking off the equivalent of 600 sheep *via* protected territory. Both matters were taken up as cross cases, and of the 1,000 sheep the whole were realized partly by those brought in by the thieves, and partly by a barampta on the Nana Khels made by the Mahsuds themselves. As regards the 600 sheep taken by Kashmir, these ought properly to have been restored by him to Samandar, but the latter said be was so grateful for the way he had been avenged that he would let them stay where they were.

118. There are of course always cattle going off from the unprotected area, but in many of the cases from the protectorate the Wazirs are themselves to blame. They absolutely neglect to send out with their flocks an armed man of any kind, and as a result a couple of unarmed Mahsuds passing cannot resist the temptation, and go off with a few sheep. In such cases it is well to recover the sheep to discourage theft, but to give them to the Militia. With the marked protectorate the Militia posts have each their

circle to patrol and watch, and any charge must be reported on by the Native Officer or NCO Commanding the Post, so that no thefts should occur and no charges come into protectorate which are really independent territory.

May 1903.

# Appendix-I

(Sketch—Not printed.)

The present map, which makes no pretence at accuracy of proportion, will give a very fair idea of the present distribution of Spin. The whole partition of the main plain is done by four land marks.

The main line joins the Ghalipon. Warsak on the north, with an unnamed small warsak to the south, which is easily recognized by a waiving black line running right down it. This line passes about 200 yards to the west of Spinkot. To the east the boundary is the water in the Dargai Algad. The third is a line running east and west from the north wall of the Spinkot.

The partition in Kotina cannot be mistaken.

The parts still undivided are:

Sui Narai

Angar Khulla

Kotina Raghza

Spin Tangi

Spin Tangi is a vague term, and may include land in the Upper Dargai Algad. The test is—any land on which the pakka water of the Algad can be brought is comprised in Spin Tangi and is joint. There is a piece of land at the spot marked $A$ on the map to the west of the water. This was claimed by the Sheikh Bazid as joint. It was finally decided that this should be allowed to remain with the Kaka Khels, but that they and the Utman Khels should give the Sheikh Bazid Khels one-third of the area of this land up above. They probably will forget to do so, but the quantity is so small comparatively that it really does not matter. The point $B$ is a small piece of joint land reserved for a Sheikh Bazid kot.

The main points to note about the partition are:

(1) The Sheikh Bazid Khels have   360 shares

    The Utman Bazid Khels have   290   "

    The Kaka Bazid Khels have   280   "

The Utman Khel have 320 shares, of which the Khandi Khels have 56. The remaining 264 shares are again divided into 270, of which the Abkar Khels, Shahdar Khan, have 6.

(2) Water rights are in the same proportion.

The Utman Khels claim 300 shares, but this is probably illusory.

The Kharri water is divided from the Kaka Khels' land, but this gives them no claim to regulate the division. All Kharri water is joint, and is divided in the same proportion.

(3) The present Spinkot is the property of the Utman Khels. They have full right to knock it down, but should one Utman Khel place a hut in it, the whole section will have to pay the other two one-half of the cost.

# Appendix-II

## Four Cases

### (1) Miedaka land

*Miraband, Kikarai; Pir Muhammad, Masti Khel; Mirza Gul.*—This land was the property of Kikarais. They wanted to sell it to Mirza Gul. Pir Mohammad, etc., claimed:

(1) that the land was theirs;
(2) that they had right of pre-emption.

They finally abandoned claim (1).

Mirza Gul was prepared to pay Rs. 1,700 Kabuli for this land. Pir Muhammad said the price was excessive.

The Kikarais nominated Galazan, Ashraf Khel.

The Masti Khels nominated Awali, Yar Gul Khel.

These first of all gave to the Kikarais a small piece of land about which there was a dispute. They then fixed the value of the land at Rs. 1,400 Kabuli to be paid in cash alone, and gave the Masti Khels three months to pay. If they fail to do so within that time, they can only exercise their pre-emption for Rs. 3,000 Kabuli or the Kikarais may sell it to any one they like. Of the present crop the Kikarais are to receive one-sixth.

Finding accordingly.

18.4.03.                                                                                      F. W. J.

---

### (2) Qadir and Zangi.

On Ghoikwha side is a small piece of ground claimed by Qadir and Zangin

The land was originally the property of Zangin and Sherdad and Qadir. Bannocha states that years ago he made the partition, giving Sherdad and Zangin equal measurements. Sherdad's boundaries are fixed. Their length B C is 183 yards. A B is also 185 yards. D A is 40 yards. It would therefore appear on first sight that Qadir is right. But C E is undoubtedly much broader than A F, and Zangin claims that for that reason he got more, *viz.*, D B.

15-4-03.                                                                                      F. W. J.

---

*(3) Sher, Nandar, Gul Ahmad.*

The Lower Ghoikho wial takes off from the Toi by Sher's Chinigai land. The case has been previously settled by Mr Grant, who divided this water into 42 waqts, of which Sher was to receive 2 for the Chinigai land. The Ghoikho owners now complain that Sher has narrowed this wial, so that it cannot carry rain floods, and that he has dug down his own land so much below the wial that percolation ensues and robbery is easy.

He has also carried across underneath it a small wial from his upper land on the right bank of the wial, which takes much of this water. Sher, on the other hand, contends that by an order of Mr Watson he was allowed to use his 2 waqts on his Ghoikho lands. Nandar, etc., deny this, saying that these waqts are only for Chinigai, and that anything which Sher does not use goes down below.

The darra containing 42 slits made by Mr Grant is still in existence, and is now twice as broad as the wial. The wial is also such as to bear out the allegations above.

15-4-03.                                                                F.W.J.

This dispute ended in a fight:
  Mirza Gul
  Sher's son Sherabat     } Went to jail.
  Khidr Khan
The dispute is possibly ended.

J.B.B.

*(4) Kuli lands.*

These lie up towards Pirghwaza and Torghwaza from Ghoikho. Water can only be carried on to them from the highest wial of all. The lands are claimed by the Boki Khels, who say they reclaimed them. The entire quantity is very vast, and that reclaimed by the Boki Khels is small in proportion. There are undoubted signs of their having cleared the land, raised dams, made a rain ditch, etc., but they have probably not touched them for four or five years. Their claim to the entire tract is ludicrous.

The claimants now are:
(1) Bannocha, who claims to have reclaimed these before the Boki Khels. (This claim need not be considered.)
(2) The Boki Khels.
(3) The Ghoikho owners.
(4) The Zilli and Taji Khels jointly.

15-4-03.                                                                F.W.J.

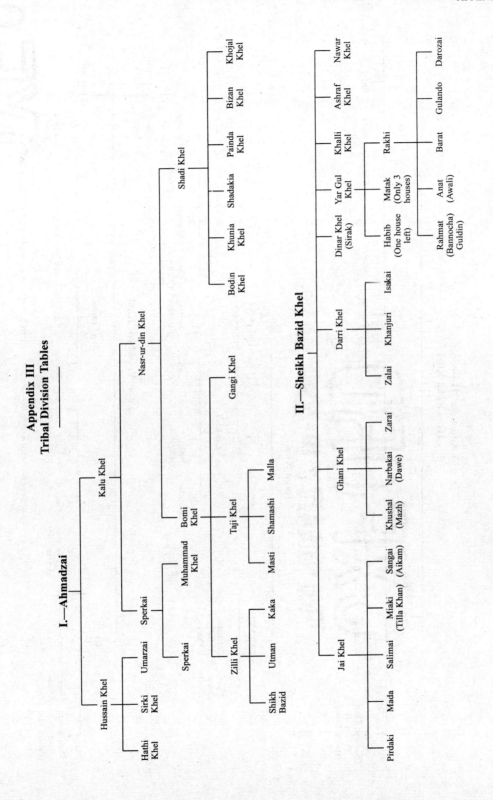

**Appendix III**
**Tribal Division Tables**

**I.—Ahmadzai**

**II.—Sheikh Bazid Khel**

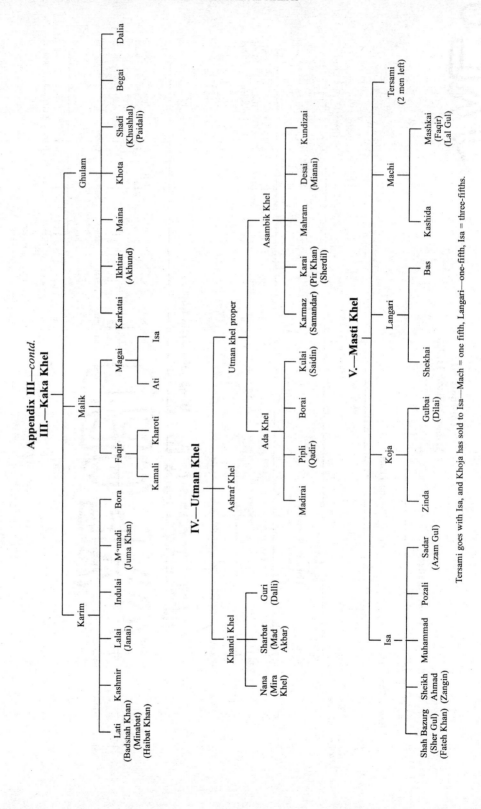

**Appendix III—contd.**
**III.—Kaka Khel**

**IV.—Utman Khel**

**V.—Masti Khel**

Tersami goes with Isa, and Khoja has sold to Isa—Mach = one fifth, Langari—one-fifth, Isa = three-fifths.

**Appendix III**—*contd.*

## VI.—Shamshi Khel

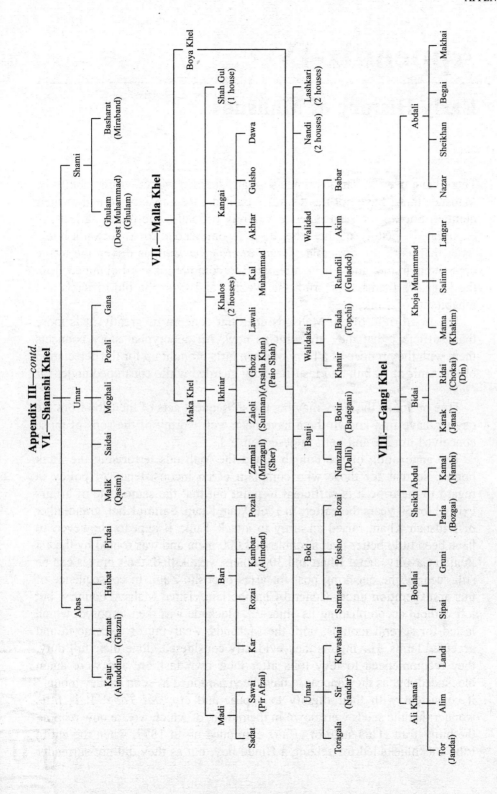

## VII.—Malla Khel

## VIII.—Gangi Khel

# Appendix-IV

## Early History of Mahsuds

There have been at various times so many learned works written about the Mahsuds that I have not the desire, even had I the capacity, to add to their number. Should the reader desire a purely official—one might almost say expurgated—history of the tribe, he is recommended to Anderson's book. After that work the principle of *audi alteram partem* has driven me to the opposite extreme, and I have attempted to compile a record obtained from the Mahsuds themselves, from the Wazirs, and from the old officials and inhabitants of Tank.

The first origin of the Mahsuds does not concern us greatly; it is more than sufficient that they are with us now. An apocryphal story connects them with the produce of a bevy of slave girls brought up for the delectation of the Amir of Kabul, and insufficiently guarded while encamped under Pir Ghal.

True or not as the story may be, the subsequent acts of the tribe from the day we have first known them have been well worthy of the sons of those conceived in rape and born in desertion.

The annexation of the Punjab found the Mahsuds terrorising the Tank border, so that for those who complain of an inconsistency of policy in regard to the tribe it is sufficient to point out that the same state of affairs existed for 50 years thereafter. In 1860 Jangi Khan, Salimi Khel, grandfather of Badshah Khan, raised an army to attack Tank. It appears, however, to have been little better than a rabble of 3,000 men, and was routed by the 1st Punjab Cavalry. Jangi Khan and 300 others were killed: their graves can be still seen by the checking post for arms opposite Zam. In consequence of this an expedition under General Chamberlain visited Mahsud country, but left without accomplishing its object. A blockade was then imposed, which lasted for several months, until the Mahsuds, wearying of it, came in and accepted terms. Having, as they evidently considered, done their full duty, they recommenced to levy tolls after their own fashion, and were again blockaded; but as they appear to have been pardoned as soon as they thought it consistent with their dignity to appear and cry *Hai Toba*! It is little wonder that the seeds were sown in them then, of which we are now reaping the bitter fruit. This state of affairs continued up to 1877, when the entire tribe was blockaded for seizing a Hindu boy; but as they did not surrender this boy until after they had been under blockade for over six months, it is perfectly obvious that, as they could care nothing for the boy, they cared uncommonly little for the blockade. In the meanwhile the entire government of the tribe had been conducted from the very start of our rule through the Nawab of Tank, who appears to have been a local potentate of very considerable powers. The result, it must be admitted, had done him and his predecessors very little credit. From 1873 onwards the Deputy Commissioner of Dera, Major Macaulay, began to take the management of affairs out of his hands. The Nawab's powers were gradually encroached on, until finally in 1879 matters reached a crisis, when the Nawab was put in gaol and his son blew out his brains.

Local opinion is still divided on the rights and wrongs of this matter. Some say the Nawab was discovered in fraud, and others that it was entirely the work of the Nawab's reader, who put up a forgery under the Nawab's seal at the instigation of Azim Khan, Kundi, who even then had loomed over the horizon of Mahsud affairs.

The Nawab anyway at Lahore was dissatisfied with his position and sent letters to Mashak, Abdur Rahman Khel, Barak, Langar Khel, and Umar Khan, Salimi Khel, Mahsuds, as well as to leading Bhittanis and Wazirs, inviting them to protest in the usual manner against his detention.

It was accordingly decided to protest, but, as it happened, there was at Dera a troup of hostages, who according to the custom of the time, were periodically being taken and released. These hostages were informed of what was going on, and put in a petition asking to be removed to Tank, as the air there was much more favourable to their health. This was granted, and the hostages arrived in Tank. Everything now being ready, the Mahsuds moved down from their hills, burnt Tank quietly, and departed with their hostages.

The date of this, 1879, is a land mark in Mahsud history, and useful to mark Mahsuds' ages by; also to point a double moral.

In case it may be of interest, the sons of these leaders are in evidence today. They are Alam Gul and Kastor, Abdur Rahman Khels; Salahin, Langar Khel; Badshah Khan, Salimi Khel.

In consequence of this the inevitable punitive expedition went out in 1881, but as it confined its efforts to the Nana Khels, and even then left without accomplishing its object, it is not to be wondered at that the Mahsuds were beginning to regard punitive expeditions as little more troublesome than house flittings.

Finally, after a blockade the six men demanded were surrendered, but as the survivors were released four years later, the moral effect cannot have been great.

After this things appear to have run on more or less in the usual way, and as the Mahsuds were more moderate in their depredations, no special measures were taken.

In 1887, the question of opening the Gomal was taken up by Mr Ogilvie's setting out from Murtaza to Nili Kach with a considerable Tank following— 300 Mahsuds and Azim Khan, Kundi. Near Nili Kach there was lying a Darwesh Khel kirri, which the Mahsuds, strong in their position as friends of Government, took upon themselves to raid. Thereupon a fight took place, in which the Wazirs were finally worsted and took refuge in Mr Ogilvie's camp. The matter ended there for the time, but when darkness fell a few Mahsuds, who considered that neutrality had been violated, spent the night sniping the camp. This was at the time supposed to have been done by Jambil, Abdur Rahman Khel, but better accounts agree in attributing it to Alibat, Garrarai, who fell at Wana in 1894. The damage done, however, was not serious, one horse belonging to Azim Khan, Kundi, being the total bag.

Next day, when the exploring party proposed to return, it was found that the malcontents held the hills on the Murtaza road. The party accordingly turned off down the Sheranna and came out at Manjhi, and spent the night in Gomal Bazar. Even then the malcontents would not let them have their night in peace.

The action taken by Government in consequence of this inhospitality affords a curious side light on the position of hostages, who, as we have already seen, were being periodically taken and released.

Since 1881, 80 hostages had been entertained at Rs. 12 a month each, and now on account of the misbehaviour of their brothers and cousins these unfortunates were to be deprived of their unearned increment and sent back to their hills to earn what scanty maintenance they could steal from the people of Tank. As a counterpoise to this Jambil, who was credited with the leadership of the malcontents, was made a Malik, doubtless on the principle, which led to so much trouble later, of 'reconciling the malcontents'.

In 1888, Mr Bruce arrived, and shortly thereafter took place the great Appozai jirga, in which the allowances of the Mahsuds and Wazirs were first put on a clear basis. Sir Robert Sandeman made a tour from Zhob down the Gomal to Tank by Kajuri and Nili Kach with great success.

The posts of Kajuri Kach, Nili Kach, Spinkai Kach and Kashmiri Kar were put in hand. These posts were to belong to the Shaman Khel, Manzai, Bahlolzai, and Mianis, respectively, to be held by their levies. Khuda Bakhsh and Fazl Haq were appointed the subordinate officers, with J. Donald over them at Tank. At this time the Mahsuds were evidently in no state for overt acts. Disapproving generally of these posts, which were being rapidly completed by Mahsud labour, they did not dare to attack them themselves, but put up the Wana Ahmadzais to attack Kajuri. These came down in great strength, but were beaten off by Said Akbar Shah, Sinobar Shah, and his relatives. This is the only good thing I ever heard of Said Abkar Shah's having done, and I am glad to be able to mention it.

Meanwhile there can be no doubt that with the Mahsuds occupied building posts and obtaining allowances there was a distinct lull on the Tank border. As my chronicler says, a spirit of conciliation was abroad of which the Mahsuds were availing themselves to their own aggrandisement. I quote the words of the chronicler without prejudice and without any guarantee of their truth:

'When these people were made chief Maliks then the palms of others began to itch, and by committing offences in Government territory they too became Maliks. Haji Muhammad, Shaman Khel, left the jirga in a rage because he was a Malik of only Rs. 5. Just outside the west gate of Tank he came upon a faqir whom he killed. Then Mr Bruce made him a Malik of Rs. 10.

'Jaggar Abdur Rahman Khel, began to make raids in Zhob, and did a considerable amount of damage. He was promised a Maliki if he would desist, which he did. It was Khuda Bakhsh Khan who arranged this kindness for him, and the way he repaid it will be told later.

'At the end of the Tank Jirga Azmat, Bathai, and Ata Muhammad, Kai Khel, carried off a Hindu *halwai*, and were made Maliks for restoring him. Badr Din got together a party of men and rifles, and frightened the other Maliks into recommending him for a second class Maliki.

'The Brumi Khels raised a gang and destroyed the works on the Tank Zam, which had been recently erected at great expense. Accordingly Shali was made a Malik. It was Shali's son. Sabir, who stole the guncotton, but that is another story. It was for bringing this same Shali into Tank on time to answer for his offence that Muhammad Afzal became a second class Malik.

'Bakhsari, Garrarai, and Aib Khan raided a Bhittani village in British territory and killed 4 men. When they were called upon to answer for their misdeeds, they said they wanted to be Maliks. Accordingly they were made Maliks.

'When Jambil and Jaggar were made Maliks all the Abdur Rahman Khels began to raid. Accordingly every house-holder was made a Malik.

'Alim Khan, Kai Khel, being annoyed, destroyed the road between Nili and Spinkai. He was made a Malik of Rs. 5. Khatkai Malikshai as a protest destroyed the trees in the Tank garden. When the news got out he was made a Malik of Rs. 10.

'Shawar Din, Nazar Khel, was made a Malik for setting fire to the grass stored by the Commissariat in Tank.

'Mamak, Shingi, got his Maliki of Rs. 10 by kidnapping a Hindu from Bannu.'

1892.—The position of affairs now was that the Gomal was held up to Kajuri and the Zam to Khirgi, but so far no advance had been made either in the direction of Wana or Jandola. It was now that the trouble with the Amir began. It seems unnecessary to enter here into any detailed story of Sardar Gul Muhammad's trips from Gul Kach to Wana to Jandola; how he set the whole country by the ears; how he objected to being addressed as 'Hifzahu;' and how he cleared out the Splitoi Abdur Rahman Khels who stole his tea. Anyway he disappeared at the end of 1892, and the Durand Agreement and the Boundary Commission followed in due course.

1893.—Meanwhile there was a considerable amount of what euphemistically might be called unrest among the Mahsuds, and this culminated with the shooting of Mr Kelly between Moghal Kot and Kajuri. But here we must tread warily, for this is the Mahsud Dreyfus ease.

The charge was first laid upon Wazirs, particularly Zariband and other Shakiwals, and a massed jirga of Wazirs and Mahsuds was held at Jandola. Finally suspicion placed its leaden feet on Jambil and Karam, Abdur Rahman Khels. After much pressure, whether financial or otherwise, an enormous concourse of Mahsuds, accompanied by Jambil and Karam as honoured guests, moved into Sheikhbudin and began substantially to disturb the peace of that salubrious station. The case was tried by jirga, and the finding, if I remember right, was that 150 Mahsuds, of whom 50 were to be Nana Khels, were to swear to Jambil's and Karam's innocence. Naturally every one knew that this would be the finding, and had solemnly promised the accused to swear to their innocence, otherwise, of course, the accused would never have dreamt of coming. Anyhow, as the official reports say, when the time for swearing came the 'Nana Khels began to waver.' As I was not there at the time I cannot say, but the story of the Mahsuds that this wavering was caused by the peregrinations of Azim Khan, Kundi, with a bag of rupees does not appear altogether beyond the dreams of imagination.

Jambil and Karam went off for seven years apiece. Dawegar, Giga Khel, the father of Muhammad Afzal, Umr Khan, father of Badshah Khan, and others were killed. Jambil and Karam are now out on three years' good security, and Jambil is working excellently.

The two of them have ascertained the rewards given to various Maliks and divided their spheres of influence, and as soon as their security is up are going to realize the money from their separate assignees.

Meanwhile Khalu had not been idle.

Qadir Bakhsh, Jemadar, the son of his old friend, who made Khalu's brother Jaggar a Malik, was a Jemadar of Levies. He pursued thieves right into the Splitoi, and put up in the house of Jaggar. While he was asleep

Khalu killed him. The Mahsuds were called upon to bring in Khalu for the slaughter. They said he was in his tower and they could not catch him, and asked for ammunition. Then, according to the historian, they received such a 'magazine' as had never before been seen in Waziristan. They again reported that Khalu was too fierce and asked to be allowed to bring him in on itbar. They did so, and he was thrown into gaol. Whereupon two sepoys were killed, and it was thought better to release Khalu before more were killed. The official chronicle says the Mahsuds were fined Rs. 3,000, but does not specify how this money was obtained. Offences were now going on in regular succession, sepoys being killed all over Waziristan, but according to the official chronicler the state of affairs seems to have culminated in a Gujar Sheranni being robbed of his rifle and bullock.

We now come to the Boundary Commission and the attack on the Wana camp. The story is too well-known to require repeating, but a perusal of the printed files will be found not uninteresting.

The point that puzzles me is Mr Bruce's notes on the causes of the attack:

(1)   The Maliks had no part in it at all.
(2)   The cause was the inequality of the allowances.

Now, as no one but the Maliks had the fingering of the allowances, who else would make (2) a cause for discontent. The fact is that the Maliks in their own bodies were undoubtedly in the camp, but their brothers, sisters, cousins, and aunts were merrily engaged in the attack.

We are told the principal sections concerned were: ...Langar Khels,...; but that Badr Din, Muhammad Afzal, Salehin, Bara Hissar, etc., were loyal.

If these men were real Maliks and really meant well, how could their section move.

The fact is that the Maliks were chosen in the most slip-shod fashion. Had a complete jirga of the Mahsuds been called in, and the Maliks properly nominated by them and the allowances been distributed ratably, there is no doubt the tribe was at that time essentially Maliki in government, and that a really good Maliki system could have been established. Instead a small clique, headed by Azim Khan, Kundi, nominated its friends as Maliks, and their pay was fixed on the most arbitrary scale. Even after 1894, when the Maliki was rearranged, the same principles continued, and the result was that we got a few nominees of a clique, some representing no one but themselves, and others full of indignation because so-called bigger men got more pay.

Take the case of Mir Ajal, first class Malik of the Nana Khels. When I had the Wakils appointed by the tribe, not even one of his own Haibat Khels would make him a Malik.

Any way, an expedition moved up: the fatuous policy of friendlies was pursued: the fine imposed was paid by assessing at a fancy price grass cut by the Commissariat in the Khaisara, and generally, so far as one can hear, the Mahsuds had a thoroughly agreeable time.

That they remained straight for so many years afterwards was solely owing to Grant, and I do not believe that any one but Grant could have done it.

Not content with having set on foot an arrangement which was fairly safe to effect its own destruction, the Commissioner tried to introduce kursi nashins, which happily fell through, but the Naskor lands on arbitrary shares were set going to provide another bone of discontent, and to afford a house of call for bad characters visiting the Daman in an official capacity. Then Grant went off, and everything went Naskor. Under the elegant system described on page 67 of the official book decrees accumulated with marvellous rapidity and I had the privilege of burning five lakhs worth of unrealized decrees on Coronation Day. Badmashi became a trade from which one could retire with a Government pension.

Finally came the Blockade. This however is recent history on which it appears unnecessary to dwell.

# PART TWO

# NOTES ON THE ADAM KHEL AFRIDIS

BY

D. Donald, Esquire

(*Recorded in 1901*)

# 6

## Notes on the Adam Khel Afridis

### Origin

Genealogical accounts passed down by their ancestors have instilled in the minds of the present generation that the Adam Khels, commonly known as the Kohat Pass Afridis, like all of their class, are descended from one Karraran, whose origin is really lost in oblivion, but of whom his descendants proudly claim that he was the bastard son of a nameless Syed and an erring princess, who to hide her shame concealed the result of her indiscretion in a 'karra' or iron vessel used for cooking. In this condition was the supposed forefather of the Afridi, the Khattak, the Wazir, and Wardak found by a Mohmand jirga which presented him to his grandfather the king, then said to have been holding court in what was then the wilderness of the present Hoti Mardan. The king on learning his history named the child Karraran and forgave his daughter her weakness. Whatever the descent and origin of the Afridi, much of which has necessarily, in a people only now merging out of a state of savagery, been consigned to oblivion, the Adam Khel can at present claim to be one of the most important of his class. Adam is said to have been the fourth son of Karraran, but according to the Hayat Afghani, in which the descents of the different Afghan races have been carefully traced, he is set down as being the grandson of Karraran's younger son Usman, nicknamed the Afrida. A story as to how he derived this name is told as follows: Some guests who were staying with Usman on a dark and cold winter's night had squatted close together round a fire and in the darkness were unable to discern who was entering the house, and challenging Usman, asked who he was; he vouchsafed the reply, 'Afrida da Khudai am,' *i.e.,* I am also one of God's created.

The other three grandsons of Usman were Oola, Aka and Miri. The first of these is progenitor of the greater Oola Khel family, better known as the Khaibar Afridis, and comprising the Mir Ahmad Khel (Malikdin-*cum*-Kambar Khel), Sepaya, Zakha Khel and Qamar Khel or Qamrai clans. The second gave his name to the clan known after him, and the third not having sufficiently prospered in life has submerged his name with that of his elder brother's, and his descendants may now be found in a sub-section of the Aka Khel clan.

## Country formerly in possession of Adam Khels

The Adam Khels had originally settlements on the Bara stream and in Maidan. From the Bara owing to their original numerical weakness they are said to have been turned out by the Zakha Khel, who claim with pride to be now in possession of their former holdings in Tora Wela on the Bara stream.

## Migratory sections

In Maidan they have been gradually squeezed by their stronger brethren into the south-west corner, the land of which is less fertile than that occupied by the Oola Khel, the stronger branch of the family. The Adam Khels, however, do not ascribe the giving up of these desirable spots to any weakness, numerical or other, but relate that in addition to their settlements in Maidan and the Bara they were in possession of land in the eastern corner of the Waran Valley, now occupied by the Aka Khel Afridis and the Utman Khel section of Daulatzai Orakzais. They used to winter in their present settlements, which comprises that hilly stretch of country lying between the Peshawar and Kohat Districts, enclosed as it were in a trapezoid, the angles of which are roughly formed at the Aimal Chabutra and Shamshatu Border Police posts in the southern portion of the Peshawar District and at the Muhammadzai Border Police post and the Shahdipur Police Station in the north and east of the Kohat District respectively. With their families, blood feuds and herds constantly increasing, they found the task of migration somewhat irksome, and they decided therefore to give up their summer quarters in Tira, and to retain and strengthen their winter quarters only. Accordingly the greater bulk of the clan is resident in this country which has been above defined, and only a small fraction of the clan now migrates to the south-west corner of Maidan. This fraction comprises the whole of the Kulla Khel sub-section of the Asho Khel section of Adam Khels, nearly the whole of the Mirbash Khel sub-division of the Ismail Khel, and fairly large portions of the Bazid Khel and Sultan Khel sub-sections of the Haibat Khel Jowakis.

## Kulla Khels

The Kulla Khels nearly all migrate to their winter settlements in 'Wuch Algada' which is a dry stony bed of a ravine about 3 miles long and about 1 broad from peak to peak of the hills by which it is hemmed in the north and south. This valley runs north to south for a very short distance and then turns to the east towards Bori Jowaki. It is about 2 miles south-east of the Aimal Chabutra post, and its habitations are chiefly cave dwellings and one small village at the northern entrance of the valley. The Kulla Khels here obtain their water-supply from wells and tanks when full. These come to their winter quarters, leaving a few men in Tira to look after their villages, every November and return about May, and even some families as late as June and July, specially if the winter rains have been abundant enough to give good crops in their own country, and on lands known as 'chariker' belonging to the villages of Adozai, Mattanni and Aza Khel of the Peshawar District which the Kulla Khels and other Pass Afridis are permitted to cultivate on the payment of 'tip'. This system of cultivation will be explained later on. A few families of this section of the clan has by long occupation obtained what is practically now a proprietary right in some lands in the village of Garhi Zaid Gul Mian, about 2 miles south of Fort Mackeson in the Peshawar District. The other migratory portions of the Jowaki clan come down into the Kohat District and take up their abode chiefly in the Borakka Valley and in the hamlets adjoining the village of Shahpur, whence, in addition to finding good grazing for their herds, they are able also to earn a fairly good living by the sale of wood and grass, the produce of the Mir Koheli Hill, which is brought in large quantities by their women folk, loaded on donkeys and bullocks, their ordinary beasts of burden. A few families which are not prevented from doing so on account of blood feuds reach as far as the Ismail Khel and Sultan Khel villages in the 'Pitao' or Southern Jowaki country, whereas straggling families of these, as well as Kulla Khels, Orakzais and other Afridis, find shelter in some of the Bangash and Khattak villages of the Kohat District.

## Adam Khel country and Darra or Kohat Pass

The country of the main divisions of the Adam Khels extends in length from the sister peaks of Ziaudin and Mehr Ali Sar on the west to the sanitorium of Cherat on the east, and in breadth from the Sargashi Ridge on the north to the Tambal Peak on the south. This tract in length may roughly be estimated at 20 miles and in breadth about 10 miles; it is intersected by valleys and shrubby glens in which are located the villages according to their different sections. Taking these valleys in accordance with their importance, I begin first with that occupied by the greater part of the Gallai section and the Akhor section of the Hussan Khels. This valley is known as the 'Darra' or Kohat Pass. Commencing from its western extremity occupied by the Bosti Khel sub-section of the Gallai, it runs eastward to the first 6 miles through Bosti Khel and Sherakki country to a point known as 'Sanda Basta', where it treads due north for a mile in country occupied partly by Sherakhis and partly by the Talim Khel, Shpalkaiwal and Miri Khel sub-sections of the Zarghun Khel to the 'Shahidi Talao', whence it again bends north for 4 miles through country belonging to the Mohamad Khel, Mulla Khel and Qasim Khel sections of the Zarghun Khel to a point called 'Palosin', from which point it now turns to the north for 4 miles through country occupied by the Akhorwals to Aimal Chabutra which may be considered as the limits of the Adam Khel Afridis in this direction. Into this main valley run in three minor ones, two from the west, one occupied chiefly by the Sooni Khel sub-section of the Zarghun Khels, and the other by the Bolaki Khel and Pirwal Khel sub-sections of the Akhor (Hussan Khels), and the third from the east occupied by the Kooiwals, a younger branch of the Tor Sapar or Yaghi Khel section of the Gallai. Of the first two, the Sooni Khel glen meets the Darra about midway near 'Zara Mela' which was a village formerly occupied by a mixed population of Sherakki and Zarghun Khel and is now held by a few families of 'karigars' or blacksmiths who are under Zarghun Khel protection. The other meets the main valley near the Peshawar entrance of the pass. The third from the east runs into the 'Darra' near 'Sanda Basta' and almost opposite the spot near which runs in the Soni Khel Valley. This main valley or darra is about 14 to 15 miles in length, and in breadth at its broadest point near the Bosti Khel limits is about ³/₄th of mile. It is occupied as aforesaid by all the sections of the Gallai, with the exception of the Tor Sapari or Yaghi Khel, and by the Akhorwal section of the Hussan Khels.

## Tor Sapar

As in the general remarks, *re* fighting population, trade and means of livelihood of the people of this tract, the Tor Saparis will have to be included, I consider it will be advisable here to give a short description of their country before proceeding on these remarks. The Yaghi Khel or Tor Saparis, a section of the Gallai, occupy a table-land to the east of the Kohat Pass. This table-land lying between two parallel ridges of hills shoots off eastward from a point about midway of the pass where the hills which form its southern boundary converge with those which form its northern. The country is really a depression between two hills of an average altitude of between 4 and 5,000 feet, and from its general appearance and formation inclines one to the belief that in pre-historic times it must have been a lake. The Tor Sapar table-land is about 2¹/₂ miles in length and about a mile in breadth. It is the healthiest and most fertile part of the Adam Khel country. It is reached from the Shahidi Talao *viá* the Shpalkai Kandao, the ascent over which is steep and rugged, but laden bullocks, mules and donkeys use the road regularly, and I once rode a 14-2 horse up it without having to dismount. On the Tor Sapar side there is practically no descent. The land is all irrigated from wells found at an average depth of some 15 feet from the surface.

## Physical Features

The physical features of this tract are best described by saying that it is a country of rugged mountains rising in some cases to an elevation of 6,500 feet and stony ravines. The hills are sparsely wooded with a growth of shrubs and stunted trees, chiefly the ilex oak, wild olive, palosin (kikar) and a thorny bush known as the goorgoora. The oak bears small acorns and the olive and goorgoora small black unpalatable berries, which are collected for sale and consumption by the people. As often as not in the collection of the berries of the latter serious affrays take place. In good seasons there is also an abundance of grass in these hills which is mostly cut and stacked for sale in Kohat and Peshawar by the Afridi women. The land, with the exception of the tracts in the Tor Sapar country which is under well irrigation and a few acres in Sooni Khel and Akhor limits watered from springs and wells respectively, is dependent for its cultivation entirely on the rainfall. Wheat, barley and bajra (millet) are its common products, though melons not of a superior quality are also grown in many parts. The produce of these fields with the exception of the melons is as a rule kept for home consumption and is rarely if ever sold.

| | | |
|---|---|---:|
| 1. | Bosti Khel | 250 |
| 2. | Sherakki | 350 |
| 3. | Sooni Khel | 100 |
| 4. | Shpalki | 30 |
| 5. | Zarghun Khel | 500 |
| 6. | Kooiwal | 60 |
| 7. | Tor Sapar | 500 |
| 8. | Akhorwals | 500 |
| | Total | 2,290 |

The total population of this area is about 10,000 souls and its fighting strength about 2,300 (see box). These subsist on the product of the land and hills, the wood and grass of which is sold in Kohat and Peshawar by the trade in salt, of which commodity they are by far the largest carriers in proportion to their population. The majority of them, however, confine themselves to the disposal of the article in the nearest market which is Peshawar, but a few of the Zarghun khels and Sherakkis who are the owners of large droves of camels go as far as Bijaur and Swat, and until very recently, when the Amir prevented the import of Indian salt into his dominions, went as far as Kabul. A great part of the population, and amongst these are some of the most respectable men now in the pass, earn a very decent and lucrative living by practising the trade of usurers. They openly discredit the calling and will tell you of untold woes which are in the world to come, to fall on the heads of such evil doers, but there is not a man amongst them who will hesitate to lend you a rupee (if he has one) in the hope of safely making two within a month or two of lending it. In regard to such loans there is a custom in vogue of washing the money in milk before paying it out, and it would seem that this custom was borrowed from the Hindus who during the Diwali festival do the same with any money which they lend out at interest. The subsidy paid to the clan which is supposed by them to be equally divided amongst every member of their clan, male or female, is also looked upon as a source of livelihood. It is looked upon as excellent security for the repayment of loans by persons borrowing money. The creditor holds the share of the person or family borrowing the money in pledge till such time as the money is repaid with the interest due, and until the debt is cleared the creditor continues to draw the share of subsidy belonging to the debtor. Malak Khani, Zarghun Khel, who is now dead, had in this way the mortgage of the shares of the subsidy of several men of his own section of the clan as well as those of the Tor Sapar, and he therefore used to take a very keen interest in the morals of the mortgagors, lest their share in the subsidy be cut for misconduct or offences committed in the pass, when his private claims on the subsidy had to give way to the demands of Government.

## Rifles trade

A lucrative and thriving trade is also followed by certain 'karigars' or blacksmiths living in the limits of the Zarghun Khel section by the manufacture and sale of Martini-Henry and other rifles. The rifles manufactured and sold by them are of three kinds:

Firstly, rifles made up from the component parts of condemned rifles which have been broken up in Government arsenals and the pieces subsequently sold by auction as iron.

Secondly, rifles put together from pieces which have either been stolen or surreptitiously sold by subordinates employed in arsenals. These pieces include very often a complete breach-block or barrel. That most of these rifles are made from whole pieces which have leaked out from arsenals is evident from the fact that a majority of the rifles in the pass bear the condemning mark on the chamber.

Thirdly, rifles which are manufactured by themselves. The Afridi gunsmith can turn out a Martini-Henry* breach-block and barrel, but both have such a primitive and want of polish look that there is no mistaking them, and even a Waziri, who is looked upon in such matter by the Afridis as the most gullible of Pathan customers, will hesitate to spend Rs. 40 on a weapon of such parts. In the manufacture of these rifles there is no secrecy and every karigar vies with his next-door neighbour in being the first to take the enquiring European over his workshop, where he is proud and glad to show you how he turns out the different parts of the rifles. But the secret of how he procures the springs, &c., he keeps to himself. These springs are generally said to be purchased from Hindu traders in Dera Ghazi Khan.

The gunsmiths like all karigars on the Afghan Frontier started life as ordinary menials, whose business it was to repair the ploughshare and the hatchet or the cycle, by no means a lucrative job. Since they have taken to the rifle trade they have become men of substance. Hussein, who is the headman amongst them, has a most venerable and patriarchal look about him, and it would be difficult from his clear cut features, long flowing white beard and spotless garments to class him as a menial. In this garb of respectability he is said to do all the purchasing in the nick nacks of his trade in Rawalpindi and Ferozepore. The karigars have a village now of their own in Zarghun Khel limits near the 'Shahidi' tank of some 15 houses to which have flocked the skilled artizans of the village of Jungle Khel in the Kohat District, who have learnt the trade of armourers in regimental workshops. Some of these latter have started a workshop in the village of Malik Ulass, Zarghun Khel, and this concern bids fair to turn out the most prosperous of all the karigars' workshops. These men have left British territory because they did not find it lucrative enough to work as repairers of arms under the terms of an annual license, and being the skilled workmen which they are, they have considerably enlivened the trade in arms. If this trade is to receive a check the only way in which it can be done is to order these British subjects back to their homes, on pain of confiscation of their lands and property, and to prohibit their ever returning again to the pass.

**Water-supply**

For their water-supply the Passmen are mainly dependent on that collected in tanks, of which there are a fair number in the pass. In recent years, however, there has been a growing tendency in favour of wells. Within the last five years no less than four wells have been dug, of these three are in Zarghun Khel limits and one in Akhor, all near the road. The average depth

---

*Of late the manufacture of these rifles has considerably improved - D. Donald.

of these wells is about 180 feet, and in seasons of severe drought they very nearly run dry. The Bosti Khel section have tanks and an old well in 'Nasar Mela'. The Sherakkis have tanks, and when these are dry they have recourse to a spring named 'Cheengai' near Mazim Mela, and also to a perennial one in the Kooi glen. Originally they had the finest well in the country, which they now remark was for water as good as a river, but a blood-feud having broken out the party which had not easy access to the well spited the one which had, by killing a number of dogs and throwing them in to foul the water. The well having accordingly remained out of use for a considerable period fell in from the top, and the bones of the dogs and the water now lie buried under about 12 feet of mud and bricks.

## Main Roads

The main roads leading out of the pass are as follows:
The main road between Kohat and Peshawar kept up by Government.

*Kandoli Lar.*—The Kandoli road starting in the pass from Khani Mela runs over the spur of the hill after which it is named, and descends down to the Kulla Khel settlements in Wuch Algadda and then on to Fort Mackeson in the Peshawar District. This road is steep and rugged on both sides of the hill, but lightly laden bullocks can get over it.

*Narai Lar.*—From the Shahidi tanks runs passed the Karigar Mela and crosses the Kandoli Ridge, a little to the east of the Kandoli Lar to 'Wuch Algadda'. It is said to be a little more practicable than the Kandoli Lar.

*Khwangai Lar.*—After passing the Karigar Mela it runs parallely east of the Narai Lar, and is said to be by far the easiest of the three which cross into Wuch Algadda. On account of its shortness Tor Sapar caravans on their way to Peshawar prefer this road to the main one in the pass, *i.e.,* when they are not on hostile terms as at present with the Kulla Khels living in Wuch Algadda.

*Shpalkai Kandas.*—This road leads as aforesaid to the Tor Sapar country from the pass. It is steep on its western face, but there is no descent on the Tor Sapar side.

*Kooi Lar.*—Through the small valley occupied by the Kooiwals an easy road leads to the Jowaki village of Jammu. On approaching Jammu the road is a bit difficult in the Nara Khula where huge boulders and slippery stones have to be got over.

*Zangi Lar.*—This road starts from the village of Nazim Mela or Sanda Basta in the pass, and leads to Kohat *via* the village of Sheikhan. On the Pass side it is easy and practicable, but on the southern or Kohat side it is quite impracticable for laden animals.

*Ghamkor Lar.*—This road is used by Basti Khels frequently to come into Kohat. It is steep and difficult on the Kohat side and impracticable for loaded animals.

*Ami Kami Lar.*—Runs from Basti Khel settlements to the Oblan stream in Bezoti country. It is quite impracticable on the Basti Khel side.

## Minor valleys

Before proceeding any further it will be as well to give a small account of the three minor valleys which drain into the pass, *i.e.,* the Sooni Khel, Akhor and Kooi.

*The Sooni Khel.*—The Sooni Khel Valley starts at the foot of the Bolandar, which is the name of a raised upland at the western extremity of the pass; it runs eastward for about $2^1/_2$ miles till it meets the pass at Zara Killi, Zarghun Khel. This spot was formerly the home of all the Zarghun Khels, of whom the Sooni Khel are only a sub-section. Finding it more profitable to move out ontowards the main road the stronger sections gradually settled down in their present holdings near the road and left the Sooni Khels in undisputed possession of their old settlements. There is a spring at the head of the valley which is capable of being used to a small extent for cultivating purposes. For the rest the valley is very much like the rest of the country, except that on the hills on its western boundary the dwarf palm or 'mazri' grows, which would be a good source of revenue to the Sooni Khels, if all the Zarghun Khels as well as other Pass Afridis, did not claim and enjoy an equal right with the Sooni Khels to cut and sell it.

*The Akhor.*—This is more or less the dry bed of a stream extending from the Ziaudin Gakha which marks the boundary between the Utman Khel Orakzais and Akhor Afridis, as well as forms the water-shed between the drainage which runs into the Mastura stream and the dry stream which traverses the whole length of the Kohat Pass. Just before this valley meets the Kohat Pass, it expands to a very small extent, and the lands here are capable of irrigation from the few wells which have been excavated. Originally all the sections of the Akhorwal lived in this ravine, but by an arrangement in 1867, after the settlement of the pass internecine quarrels, a grant of the Kalamsadda lands was made to the Gadda Khel and Bolaki Khel sub-sections. The Gaddia Khel went out to 'Kalamsadda' *in toto* and the Bolaki Khels only in such sufficient numbers as to make it unlikely for the Gaddia Khel hereafter to assume unto themselves the command of the road leading to Peshawar. In Akhor now there are only the Bolaki Khel and Pirwal Khel sub-sections. This valley commands a not over-frequented route leading from Peshawar over the Ziaudin Gakha into Utman Khel country on the Mastura and so on to Tira.

*Kooi.*—This is a small ravine which starts at the foot of the hills which divide the Tor Sapar Valley from the rest of the pass. It, contrary to the two glens above mentioned, runs from east to west and drains into the pass near 'Sanda Basta' or practically opposite the spot where the Sooni Khel Valley runs in. The Kooiwals, who are a younger branch of the Tor Sapar family, are so called because they live in the valley known as Kooi. The name Kooi is given because of a natural depression in the stream which always holds an abundance of water like a 'kooi' or well. The valley contains about four villages and is fertile, and derives its importance from being in possession of a permanent water-supply. In seasons of severe drought all the sections of the Pass Afridis, with the exception of Akhor, have to depend upon this 'kooi' for their water-supply.

## Feuds

All the different sections of the Gallai and Akhor maintain a hostile attitude towards the Jowakis. The feud was originally occasioned by petty thefts and robberies committed by one against the other. During the Jowaki Campaign in 1877 the Pass Afridis afforded asylum to refugee Jowakis, but the refuge granted was given with bad grace.

The Mohamad Khel section of the Zarghun Khel has a bitter feud with the Aimal Khel section of Bosti Khels, who are now living under the protection of the Mobarak Khel section of the Sherakkis, and are practically now domiciled Sherakkis. This feud is one of very old standing, and when hostilities become active there is an inclination on the part of the whole of the Zarghun Khels to take action against all the Sherakkis. When one threatens to block the road to Peshawar and the other the way to Kohat judicious threats *re* imposition of heavy fines prevents both sections from putting their threats into execution. This feud started some 40 years ago, and is the outcome of the act of the Tamil Khel section of Zarghun Khel. Formerly a monopoly in the salt trade was enjoyed by the Pass Afridis, who brought the salt from the mines and sold it to traders from Peshawar and Kabul, who were not allowed to proceed to the mines to purchase the article themselves. Accordingly the salt was sold at varying rates in the pass. The Akhorwals who were nearest Peshawar and furthest from Kohat sold at one rate, the Zarghun Khels at a cheaper and the Sherakkis and Bosti Khels barely covered the cost of carriage from the mines. As these traders all came from Peshawar, the Akhorwals had first call on them and did not allow them to proceed any further, unless their stock of salt was exhausted, in which case they passed them on to the Zarghun Khels and so on to the Sherakkis and Bosti Khels. The Sherakkis finding that these restrictions were not very lucrative in a most enterprising manner went into Peshawar and persuaded a caravan of Kabuli Kuchis to proceed under their escort to their own country where they would get the salt cheaper. The Talim Khel section of the Zarghun Khels had a lot of salt on hand which they wanted to sell to this caravan. Not coming to any arrangement with the Sherakkis they promptly looted the kafila. A quarrel ensued, and a Zarghun Khel of the Mohamad Khel sub-section was killed, and a Sherakki of the Mobarak Khel sub-section. The upshot is that these two sub-sections of the Zargun Khel and Sherakkis continue the feud, and the Talim Khel, the *fones et origo mali*, have withdrawn from the contest and only takes part when it becomes a general affair.

The pass internecine quarrel which raged from 1862 to 1867 is a historical affair, and will be fully explained in that part of the story which deals with our relations with the tribe.

Owing to the murder of a Kaka Khel of Garhi Zaiad Gul Mian in the Peshawar District by Kulla Khels in the Kohat Pass near the Shpalkai Kandao in 1896, all the Pass Afridis rose in a body and burnt the villages of the Kalla Khels in 'Wuch Algadda'. The feat of burning the villages was a simple one, because the bulk of the Kulla Khels, it being the summer time, were away in Tira. All the sections of Gullai and Akhor were concerned in this affair, but the Kulla Khels harbour animosity against the Tor Sapars alone, for they believe that these were the promoters of the attack on their villages.

The Akhorwals have from a very long time been at feud with the Bassi Khel section of the Aka Khels, and territorial disputes have been the chief cause of the quarrel.

### Sectional responsibility on the road

The responsibility for the safety of the road is divided as follows:

Sherakki and Bosti Khel sections are responsible from the Kotal as far as Sanda Basta.

The Tor Sapor clan is responsible from Sanda Basta to Shahidi Talao. They were originally responsible up to a point called 'Gatoosai', about a mile further on in the direction of Aimal Chabutra, but when in the new subsidy they did not receive an equal share they declined a part of their responsibility and the Zarghun Khels relieved them of it, for the road between Shahidi Talao and Gatoosai runs close by numerous Zarghun Khel villages, and the occupants of these feel themselves strong enough to accept the responsibility for the road without any extraneous help from Tor Sapar.

Zarghun Khels are responsible from Shahidi Talao to Palosin.

Akhorwals from Palosin to Aimal Chabutra. The Tor Sapars who have no land and villages near the pass used to relegate a share of their responsibility for offences committed on the bit of road told off to them to the Zarghun Khels to whom they used to pay Rs. 80 per annum as chaukidari. This chaukidari allowance to the Zarghun Khels carried the condition that if the road for which it was paid was violated, this amount would first be utilized towards the payment of compensation decreed in favour of an injured person. If the amount assessed was in excess of this amount, it came out of the Tor Sapar allowances. In the settlements between themselves which followed the acceptance by the Afridis of the construction of a good military road, the Zarghun Khels agreed in the future to forego this chaukidari allowance of Rs. 80 per annum.

The following is a brief account of the different sections:

## Basti Khel

This section lives at the western head of the valley. In all matters it has an equal share with the Sherakkis, the two sections being the descendants of two brothers. The Bosti Khel receive a total subsidy now of Rs. 1,215 per annum including the amount added on account of the construction of a good military road through the pass. This amount they divide into eight equal shares amongst themselves. They are much beset with inter-family quarrels, and one whole sub-section or kandi known as the Unas Khel have been treacherously banished from their homes and are now exiles in the Kohat District. They are constantly fighting amongst themselves, and it is possible that the prediction of a Bazoti Mullah that this section of Adam Khels would be exterminated will come true. The Mullah prophesied this when the Bosti Khels, regardless of all decency in the prosecution of a blood-feud, looted and set fire to anything they were unable to take away, which they found stored in Bazoti Ziarat. The fighting strength of this section is estimated at about 250 men; this does not include the exiles living in Kohat.

## Sherakki

*The Sherakki* as said above are closely connected with the Bosti Khel. They receive an annual subsidy of Rs. 1,215, which they divide in equal shares between the Mobarak Khel and Bash Khel sub-divisions—the former of these two gives one-third of its half-share to the Aimal Khel and Darma Khel sub-sections of Bosti Khels domiciled in their midst. The Sherakkis also have a few families living in and about the Kohat Cantonments who have been expelled from their country on account of blood-feuds. Their fighting strength is estimated at 350 men, and they have the reputation of being the most turbulent of all the Pass Afridis.

### Yaghi Khel or Tor Saparis

*Yaghi Khel or Tor Saparis.*—This section which claims descent from Gallai's eldest son would have been the strongest of all the sections if unanimity had been its lot in life. They are fairly strong now and can muster a fighting strength of some 500 men, but a great part of their population has on account of blood-feuds and other reasons drifted out of the country. The villages of Razgir Banda, 8 miles from Kohat on the Khushalgarh road, is entirely occupied by Tor Saparis, who settled there prior to our occupation of the Punjab, for Sahabdin, the son of the founder of the village, a man of about 55 years of age, states that he was born in Razgir Banda. Several other families of the portion of the clan have settled near and about the village of Shahpur near Kohat. This section enjoys a subsidy of Rs. 1,200 per annum, which after paying a small ¼th share to the Kooiwals they divide into two equal shares between the Nekzan Khel and Feroz Khel sub-sections, who again further sub-divide into small shares for each particular 'kandi'. The Tor Saparis have a reputation for being hardworking, and of all the Gallai they alone engage in manual labour in British territory to any appreciable extent. They are mostly engaged, however, in the carriage of wood and grass into Peshawar.

### Zarghun Khel

*The Zarghun Khel.*—I look upon this as the strongest and most important section at present in the pass. They occupy with the Sherakki the central portion of the valley and number about 500 to 600 fighting men, including the Sooni Khel. Their chief strength lies in their unanimity. They fight and haggle amongst themselves, but brook not the interference of others in their affairs. It consists of live main sub-sections, *i.e.,* Muhammad Khel, Miri Khel, Mullah Khel-*cum*-Kasim Khel, Sooni Khel and Talim Khel. The last-named section was in the seventies the strongest, headed by Malak Gholam; it is now the weakest, and its place in the section has been taken by the Muhammad Khel Kandi, which is by far the strongest both in point of numbers and in wealth. The Shpalkaiwals are a minor dependent division of the Zarghun Khel; they are like the main branches descendants of Yar Ali, but their great ancestress Dama, who was Yar Ali's second wife, was a 'dooma' or dancing girl, which accounts for her offspring not having prospered in life. Similarly, the Talim Khel section are not true Zarghun Khel. Their ancestor is said to have been a 'Teli' who came and settled in the pass from Bhanamari in the Peshawar District, and the name of the sub-section is derived from the trade or calling of the ancestor. Their former subsidy of Rs. 950 is divided into five equal shares between the five sections above mentioned. The Shpalkaiwals draw a separate subsidy of Rs. 60 from the confiscated Jowaki and Bangash subsidy as will be hereafter explained, and from the same source a dak allowance of Rs. 60 per annum is paid to Malik Sattar, son of Malik Gholam, Talim Khel, and a similar amount to Maliks Feroze, son of Khani (dead), Noazi and Ulassi, Muhammad Khels. Their old allowances may therefore be computed at Rs. 1,130. To this has been added Rs. 1,000 on account of the construction of the new road. Regarding the division of this new amount there has been considerable controversy and friction amongst the section of the clan. Maliks Feroze, Noazi and Ulassi, Muhammad Khels, arguing that as the new road for the greater part passes through the limits of this particular sub-section, and as they are numerically the strongest, they should take the lion's share in the new amount.

The other sub-sections fought hard to oppose this claim on the part of the three Maliks, but to no purpose. These three got their way and the arrangement finally arrived at was that a mashrana or headman's allowance of Rs. 120 was set apart for the three Maliks,* and the balance of Rs. 880, after deducting the sixth share for lungis or malikana, was to be divided amongst the four sub-sections Talim Khel, Miri Khel, Mullah khel-*cum*-Kasim Khel and Muhammad Khel; they did not propose to admit the Sooni Khel to any share, for they argued that they lived off the road like the Tor Sapars and the Shpalkaiwals; they urged they had never considered as entitled to any share. I, however, after some talking prevailed on them to pay these two sections honoraria of Rs. 40 and Rs. 20 per annum respectively.

**The Akhorwals**

The *Akhorwals* are descendants of the Barkai, Totkai and Nur Malak sub-sections of the Hassan Khel family. The Gaddia Khel who own two shares in the sections (Akhor are descended from Barkai, the Bolaki Khels who hold equivalent shares claim descent from Totkai, and the Pirwal Khel who own one share are the offspring of Nur Malik). Of their original subsidy of Rs. 2,250, Rs. 400 were allotted to the Eastern Hassan Khel after the settlement of the 'Pass internecine quarrels' in 1867; the balance of Rs. 1,850 they divide in the shares given above, *i.e.,* Gaddia Khel two shares, Bolaki Khel two shares, and Pirwal Khel one share. In the new allowances for the construction of the road they were given Rs. 750 per annum, and this amount they also divide in the same way as their former allowances. They refused to apportion any part of this for malikana. Their fighting strength is estimated at 500 men, and there is a growing tendency on the part of many members of this section, from a closer association with Peshawar, to indulge

---

*Malik Feroze, Malik Noazi and Malik Ulassi.

in gambling. An increasing trade in the sale of women by some of the younger members of the Akhorwals is much to be deprecated. The Akhorwals like the rest of the Hussan Khels strike one as being better off than the rest of the Pass Afridis. They own about six villages on the Kalamsadda lands outside the Peshawar entrance to the pass, and about five in Akhor proper.

## Political relations

As in the Khaibar so in the Kohat Pass the Afridis had been in the habit of charging tolls against all travellers and traders who used their highways. When the Governors of Peshawar serving under the Durani Amirs of Kabul took the Khaibar under their control and placed a large garrison for its protection into Ali Masjid, they found after a varied, and, it is said, expensive experience, that the Afridis were not likely to forego without a *quid pro quo* the revenues which they had derived by levying tolls, and they (Governors) were therefore compelled to offer them a fixed subsidy to compensate them for the loss of their tolls. In the Kohat Pass the Adam Khels had regularly charged tolls, and a hole scooped out in a limestone rock near the 'Zindar Tara' at the Peshawar entrance to the Pass even now marks the receptacle into which went the collections of the Afridi Collector of former days. Following the policy of the Afghan Governors in the Khaibar the British promoters of the scheme, on the annexation of the Punjab, first offered the Adam Khels a subsidy of Rs. 5,700 in 1849 for keeping open the communication of the pass (MacGregor's Central Asia, Volume II). This sum was agreed to and accepted by the Afridis, and this would seem to be the first grant of its kind made by the British Government to any of the clans on our North-West Frontier. Of this sum Rs. 3,000 were to be paid to Maliks as malikana and the balance to chaukidars.

In 1850 the Afridis attacked a party of Sappers working on the road between Fort Garnett and the Kotal. The Gallai and Akhor sections were blockaded and a threat to open out the route to Peshawar through Jowaki country made them sue for terms. In the negotiations which followed we do not seem to have scored any considerable advantage, for in addition to restoring to the Afridis their allowance of Rs. 5,700 we also engaged to pay the Orakzai Chief a subsidy of Rs. 8,000 for which he engaged to keep a hundred armed men on the Kotal Ridge for the safety of the pass. Seeing so much money pass into the hands of a man who was not of their own class, the jealousy of the Afridis was roused, and in October 1853 they attacked and captured Rahmat Khan's post on the Kotal in which it was found that there were 20 only of the 100 men whom the Orakzai Chief stipulated to keep up. The usual procedure followed, the pass was closed and the Afridis blockaded. Several schemes for a new control over the pass were proposed, but the one proposed by Colonel (then Captain) Coke was accepted, and he was directed to return to Kohat from Peshawar *viá* the Mir Kalan Pass, east of Cherat, and take action on his proposal. His suggestion practically was to transfer the control of the Pass to the Bangash clan from the Orakzai Chief whose management had been found to be not only weak but also corrupt. After a very short trial it was found that the Bangash by themselves were unable to bring the Afridis to their senses, and they therefore summoned the assistance of the Daulatzai, Sepaia and Jowaki clans, who promised their help for a consideration. The following sums were offered in subsidies: The Bangash and their Chief Rs. 3,200, Daulatzai (Bazotis and Feroze Khel) Rs. 2,000, Jowakis Rs. 2,000 and Sepaias Rs. 500 each per annum. 'Seeing this and suffering much from the blockade the Afridis tendered their submission and offered to re-open their part of the pass.' (Macgregor's Central Asia, Volume II, pages 2, 6 and 7). Their subsidy was restored, but instead of Rs. 5,700 they were in future to receive Rs. 5,400, Rs. 300 being deducted for payment to the Bassi Khel section of the Aka Khel Afridis out of the share of the Akhor subsidy. The Aka Khel share was subsequently increased to Rs. 600, the increase of Rs. 300 being met by the deduction of a similar amount from the Rs. 8,000, which used to be paid to the Orakzai Chief and which was now to be paid to the Bangash Chief, his clan and their trans-border allies. This arrangement was concluded before the end of 1853, and by it the control of the pass now vested in Bahadur Sher Khan, the Bangash Chief. The subsidies paid by Government at this time therefore were distributed as follows:

For protection of the Kotal Ridge:

|   |   | Rs. |
|---|---|---|
| 1. | Bahadur Sher Khan | 1,200 |
| 2. | Bangash clan | 2,000 |
| 3. | Daulatzai (Feroze Khel and Bazoti) | 2,000 |
| 4. | Sepaia (Muhammad Khel Orakzais) | 500 |
| 5. | Jowaki (Adam Khel Afridis) | 2,000 |
|   | Total | 7,700 |

To Pass Afridis for keeping open the communication of the pass:

|   |   |   | Rs. |
|---|---|---|---|
| 1. | Akhor (Hussan Khels) | | 2,550 |
| 2. | Zarghun Khel | | 950 |
| 3. | Tor Sapar | Sallai | 950 |
| 4. | Sherakki and Bosti Khel | | 950 |
|   | Total | | 5,400 |

Out of the Akhor Hassan Khel share the Akhorwals paid Rs. 400—in 'pasoona' voluntarily to the eastern Hassan Khel, who in return gave the assistance when required against the Bassi Khel section of the Aka Khels. In addition the Bassi Khels now began to receive an allowance of Rs. 300 which was shortly after raised by Rs. 300 more; for in 1855 we hear that their allowance of Rs. 600 was forfeited for an offence committed at the Peshawar end of the pass followed by an attack on the camp of Lieutenant Hamilton, an Assistant Engineer at Badaber. (Macgregor's Central Asia, Volume II, page 218).

These arrangements therefore resulted in no saving of money, for we paid exactly the same amount, and the only difference was that the payments were distributed over more clans and men than when the Orakzai Chief controlled the pass from 1850 to 1853.

After this, except for a short period of 26 days in 1854, the Pass remained open till February 1865. The reason why it was closed for a short time in 1854 was that a Bosti Khel Malik in the prosecution of a feud had taken the opportunity of committing several robberies, 'had plundered the pass and had refused to make restitution.' 'Major Coke on this sent the Bangash down to burn Bosti Khel and compel the inhabitants to make good the value of the plundered property and pay a fine besides.' (Macgregor's *idem*, page 217). For services in 1857 and 1858 Nawab Bahadur Sher Khan received an increase of Rs. 1,200 to his allowances, for it seems that during the troubles of the Mutiny the Pass Afridis like many of the Khaibar Afridis, instead of taking advantage of the situation and going against us, sided with us, not only by keeping quiet on their own borders, but also by supplying mercenaries to help in the restoration of law and order. To this end Bahadur Sher Khan was chiefly instrumental, and the addition made to his allowance in 1858 was looked upon as a part of the pass allowances. At the same time the Utman Khel who are an inseparable branch of the Daulatzai clan were admitted by the other two sections to a share in the subsidy of Rs. 2,000 which the Feroze Khels and Bazotis had already earned in 1853. (*vide* Aitchison's Treaties and Sanads, treaty No. 137, paragraph 5, and No. 143, paragraph 16).

The allowances in this year were as follows:

(*a*) *Kotal Allowances*

|   |   | Rs. |
|---|---|---|
| 1. | Bahadur Sher Khan | 2,400 |
| 2. | Bangash clan | 2,000 |
| 3. | Jowakis | 2,000 |
| 4. | Daulatzai (all three sections) | 2,000 |
| 5. | Sepaia | 500 |
|   | Total | 8,900 |

(b) *Road Allowances.*

|   |                   | Rs.   |
|---|-------------------|-------|
| 1.| Akhor             | 2,250 |
| 2.| Gallai            | 2,850 |
| 3.| Bassi Khel Aka Khel |  600 |
|   | Total             | 5,700 |

In 1862 started what is known officially as the Pass internecine or intestine quarrel. This was occasioned by the refusal of a Malik named Jabbar of the Akhorwals sub-section Bolaki Khel, to admit the rest of his clan to an equal division of the subsidy. Jabbar received the share of subsidy at the hands of Nawab Bahadur Sher Khan, the Bangash Chief, and claimed the right to divide it as he pleased. This gave great offence to the remaining Gaddia Khel and Pirwal Khel Maliks, who questioned his claim. Matters came to a climax when in that year, for an affront offered to a guard escorting General Chamberlain's baggage through the pass, a fine of Rs. 100 was imposed on the offenders, who all belonged to Malik Jabbar's faction. The Malik wished to distribute the fine over the whole Akhor subsidy, but the Gaddia Khels protested, and requested that it should come out of the share of the Bolaki Khels. The fat was in the fire, and shots were exchanged between Gaddia Khel and Bolaki Khel sub-sections. The former sought and obtained the assistance of the Eastern Hussan Khel and the latter therefore at once applied to the Gallai who were not slow to take part in the quarrel. Fighting in the pass took place between the parties and no attempts to bring about a reconciliation proved successful. The fighting having assumed a serious aspect, the Commissioner of Peshawar was obliged to close the pass in February 1865. (Macgregor's *idem*, page. 218). The closure of course included a suspension of their subsidies. On the 24th October 1866 a settlement was arrived at and the pass was again declared open. The terms of this settlement were as follows:

1) That the account for killed and wounded should be settled between the parties according to Afghan custom by the payment of blood-money on the usual scale.
2) That each section of Akhor should be answerable for its own expenditure, but that all should be jointly responsible for any government demand, provided that if it was clear and beyond doubt that a crime was committed solely by any particular section, that section alone should bear the fine. That the allowances should be paid at the Government treasury into the hands of the Bolaki Khel Maliks who should at once separate the shares of the other sections and pay the amounts to the representative Maliks.

69

3) That the Hussan Khel towers should be taken possession of by Government, and that the same should be held in trust for a period of at least six months by some men of the Kaka Khel under Mian Zaiad Gul, and that the Hussan Khel should never receive it back, and that it rested with Government to retain it or pull it down.

4) That the Hussan Khel should receive an annual sum of Rs. 400 as 'lungee' from the Akhor allowances payable by Government, but that they were to have no share in the pass arrangements or responsibilities.

5) That the Gaddia Khel have a right to build a meyla (hamlet) on the Kalamsadda beyond matchlock distance of the road, but that the Bolaki Khel should also build one, but beyond Matchlock Range of that of the Gaddia Khel.

6) That after the harvest the Gaddia Khel should be put in absolute possession of their former lands. The crop of the lands sown should be enjoyed by the Gullee, who should pay the Gaddia Khel the usual proprietary due.

7) That the property and cattle destroyed on either side should be considered squared.

8) That the Bassi Khel question should be reserved until the arrival of that tribe when the Government would finally decide the Khalamsadda question. (Cavagnari's Printed Memorandum, pages 46, 47 and 48).

The Hussan Khels after accepting the above terms temporarily demurred about putting No. (3) into execution, but seeing that Major Pollock, who was then Commissioner, and his colleagues intended to carry the details of the settlement through hastily the day after acceptance of the terms, removed their chaukidars and handed the tower over to Mian Zaiad Gul's men. This tower is still standing and is occupied by two men of the Eastern Hussan Khel section who are paid Rs. 3 per mensem out of Hussan Khel allowance of Rs. 400 per annum.

About this same time the Bassi Khels taking advantage of the broils into which the Akhorwals had plunged themselves resumed their claim to the 'Kalamsadda' lands and in the settlement arrived at refused, together with the Hussan Khels, to accept the terms offered to them, and in consequence had to be debarred from entering British territory on 11 February 1867. 'They, however, eventually submitted on the 8 and 24 April 1867, and the terms given to them were those originally offered, viz., that the Bassi Khel should agree to a further truce of seven years on the 'Kalamsadda' question, and in consideration of this, should receive an increase of Rs. 400 to the Rs. 600, which they formerly received as their share of the pass allowance.' (Macgregor's, page 218).

In 1870 Lord Mayo rode through the pass on his way to Kohat, and a few days after, on 15 April 1870, a servant of Captain Stainforths and two muleteers were cruelly murdered in the pass, for which offence Captain Macaulay, then Deputy Commissioner, Kohat, at once made a reprisal on Afridi animals in the district, and by the evening of the same day had Rs. 10,000 worth of Afridi property in his possession. The terms which included the destruction of the houses of the men actually concerned in the murder, with restrictions not to rebuild without the permission of Government, their expulsion from the country for one year, and a payment by each of them of a fine of Rs. 1,000 were accordingly speedily fulfilled. Nazar Ali, a Zakha Khel, who was concerned in the murder and to whom of course the above orders could not apply, was subsequently arrested in Akhor by the Adam Khels and was delivered up to justice on 7th August of the same year and was hung on 19th on the crest of the Kotal. (Macgregor's, Volume II, page 219).

In 1875 and 1876 there was a further rupture with the Pass Afridis, and the causes which led up to this were as follows:

For several years previously the Government had been considering the question of improving the communication of the pass road, and of making it practicable for wheeled traffic. This construction the Afridis, fearful of the loss of their independence, had persistently opposed. The Commissioner of Peshawar acting on the advice of the local officers at the time, who considering our relations then with the Passmen on a most friendly footing, re-opened the question in 1873. Nawab Bahadur Sher Khan also considered that there would be no serious opposition to the construction of the road. So the jirga was summoned and the assent of the different sections requested.

The Pass Afridis generally were amenable to the construction of the road, but Sherakki section stoutly opposed the measure. In order to embroil the whole tribe, they started their ordinary tactics of ill-treating and robbing travellers on the road and refusing to send in their particular jirga to give any explanation. This was shortly followed by the commission of dacoities and other serious offences in British territory, with the result that the pass had to be declared closed on 7th February 1876, and a blockade of the Pass Afridis was ordered; moreover the Afridis crops which had been grown within the British territory were declared as confiscated. We had later on the 15th April to send out a force of two cavalry regiments and one infantry and a host of our own villagers of the Peshawar District to put the confiscation into execution. (Gazetteer, North-West Frontier, page 1001). These crops were presumably grown on the Kalamsadda lands by the Akhor section of the Hussan Khels.

The Hussan Khels were the first to submit and agreed to the terms of Government, which included the construction of the road through their limits. Subsequently the Gallai also submitted and agreed to the improvement of the rocky part of the road, north of the Kotal, under Government supervision, and also to payment of a fine of Rs. 3,000, (Gazetteer, North-West Frontier, page 1002.)

From my present experience of the Kohat Pass Afridi, I am quite unable to understand the attitude of the Sherakki section in this matter. Seeing that all the other sections had practically acquiesced in, and accepted, the proposal of Government, it was quite impracticable for the Sherakkis, who after all represent only half a section, to oppose so stoutly as to embroil the whole clan in a rupture with Government. There are two solutions of the problem:

The first is that opposition was the secret wish of the whole clan and the Sherakkis, who have a reputation for being obstructionists, were asked to make scapegoats of themselves, so that in any coercive measures which followed they alone should be the objects of the Government displeasure, in which case the other sections would give what assistance they could in palliating their sufferings. It was also possible that the clan understood that Government, seeing the objection of one of the sections to the proposal, might forego their demand.

The second solution is that Nawab Bahadur Sher Khan, who was the middleman negotiating for us, had a host of enemies quite as popular and influential as himself with certain sections of the Pass Afridis living in Kohat at the time, and these latter worked the opposition of the Sherakkis to this proposal. The rupture with the Pass Afridis had only just been settled when the Jowaki hostilities commenced, one of the terms of the settlement of which was the forfeiture for the future of the Jowaki allowance of Rs. 2,000 per annum. Sir Louis (then Captain) Cavagnari reported in his letter No. 183, dated 22nd September 1877, that he proposed redistributing the pass allowance in future as follows. This redistribution was based on the assumption that the Jowaki subsidy and the allowance to the Bangash clan, amounting in all to Rs. 4,000, would be forfeited as proposed by him. No sanction of Government appears to have been received by him, but he seems to have put his redistribution into force. Accordingly he seems to have increased the Sherakki and Bosti Khel allowance by Rs. 480 per annum for improvement and protection of the road on the north side of the Kotal, which was in their limits. The increase was also assigned as the pay of 8 chaukidars at Rs. 5 per mensem each to be kept up by these two sections. These eight chaukidars have never been appointed by the Sherakki and Bosti Khel, and the two sections always maintain that the amount was only paid for the improvements to the bit of road in their limits which they carried out.

Captain Cavagnari's proposed redistribution which he put into force was as follows:

|  |  | Rs. |
|---|---|---|
| 1. | Pay of 16 Bangash chaukidars on the Kotal at Rs. 5 per mensem each | 960 |
| 2. | Pay of 8 Sherakki and Bosti Khel chaukidars | 480 |
| 3. | Allowance to Shpalkaiwal | 60 |
| 4 | Personal allowance to Gholam, Zarghun Khel, now continued to his son Sattar | 60 |
| 5. | To be paid to Akhorwal and Hussan Khel when they make new road | 600 |
| 6. | Balance to Kotkai and Shahidi Talao Serai chaukidars | 1840 |
|  | Total | 4,000 |

With reference to item No. 3, the Shpalkaiwals are a small and insignificant section of the Zarghun Khels who had not been admitted by the parent section of the clan to any share in the subsidy of Rs. 950 paid to them, and as they live very near the road, it was possibly found politic to appease them for the slur cast on them by their own people by not admitting them to a share.

Item No. 4.—Gholam, Zarghun Khel, was the Malik of the Talim Khel section of Zarghun Khels who appears to have done yeomen service for us in the pass. His son, Sattar, now draws this allowance.

Items Nos. 5 and 6 appear to have been allowed for in the redistribution scheme, but as they were conditional on the construction of a good road through the Akhor limits and the erection of serais at Kotkai and Shahidi Talao, both of which conditions were never fulfilled, it would seem they were never paid out.

The Punjab Government in their no. 2467, dated 27th July 1878, sanctioned the payment of the Bassi Khel subsidy of Rs. 1,000 by the Deputy Commissioner, Peshawar, instead of by Deputy Commissioner, Kohat.

In course of time the attention of Government was drawn to the expenditure incurred from these forfeited Jowaki and Bangash allowances amounting to Rs. 4,000, and reports were called for. Major Plowden, in his No. 295–3095, dated 19th August 1879, traced back the history of these allowances to 1st December 1853, and the above-mentioned letter is my authority for statements regarding payment and distribution of these subsidies.

As a result of the above correspondence, the Bangash subsidy of Rs. 2,000 was appropriated towards the pay of a permanent establishment on the Kotal, resulting in the expenditure of Rs. 1,566, Rs. 434 thus being saved.

Nawab Bahadur Sher Khan died in August 1880, and till May 1882 his allowance of Rs. 2,400 was continued to his brother Atta Muhammad Khan, when orders were received that the pass was to be taken under the direct control of the Deputy Commissioner and was not to remain under the management of a middleman. Accordingly the allowance paid to Atta Muhammad Khan was withheld, and the Deputy Commissioner continued to spend the money, so saved, for services connected with pass management. Several anomalies regarding such expenditure having crept in, a further report by Government as to the distribution of this money was called for in 1888 from Mr. Udny, who was then Deputy Commissioner, Kohat. This was disposed of by Colonel (then Captain) Leigh in his No. 169-1154, dated 6th April 1889, enclosing a memorandum by Sir R. (then Mr.) Udny, dated 18th September 1888, which gave a full and concise account of these allowances and the payments made therefrom. The orders of the Punjab Government were conveyed in the Chief Secretary's letter No. 380, dated Simla, 8th August 1889, which forbade for the future all unauthorized expenditure and directed that the Bangash subsidy of Rs. 2,000 was to be utilized for the entertainment of fixed and permanent establishment on the Kotal, and the allowance of Rs. 2,400 paid to the Bangash Chief was to be considered a part of the annual contingent grant at the disposal of the Deputy Commissioner for charges on account of the entertainments of jirgas and rewards for services and for unforeseen contingent charges connected with the control of the pass. It has not been mentioned before; nor do I find it stated by any of the authorities I have quoted above that the Daulatzai sections in lieu of their subsidy of Rs. 2,000 undertook to maintain 12 chaukidars on the Kotal; of these chaukidars the Feroze Khel furnished 6 and the Bazoti and Utman Khel 3 each. These men were paid at the rate of Rs. 4 each, which sum amounting to Rs. 576 was deducted annually from their subsidy for payment by the Deputy Commissioner to the chaukidars. This left a balance of Rs. 1,424, divisible among the three sections—the Feroze Khel receiving one half, and the Bazoti and Utaman Khel the balance in equal shares. The Sepaia also similarly supplied two chaukidars at the same rate of pay. These chaukidars, together with those paid from the Bangash allowance, were employed till very recently for the protection of the Kotal and its connected towers. Government of India in their No. 2495 F., dated 11th October 1900, have sanctioned the substitution of Border Military Police in place of the chaukidars, who have been done away with effect from 1st February 1901.

The Daulatzai sections and Sepaia, who have lost by this arrangement to the extent of the value of a goat (pussa) Rs. 5 due yearly from each man, are to be recouped by the payment of the same from Political Funds at the disposal of the Deputy Commissioner. The Government of India is their No. 2315 F., dated Simla, 23 August 1899, ordered the construction of a good military road through the Kohat Pass. The Deputy Commissioner, Kohat, was directed to summon the pass jirga to inform them of the wishes of Government, who wished to make this road with their acquiescence and to pay them something for their concurrence, but were prepared to make it in any case if they demurred. Accordingly these orders were announced, and the jirga after hearing them asked for 15 days' grace to discuss the matter with the rest of the clan. The day fixed for the receipt of their reply was 15th September 1899. The jirga failed to appear, but turned up the next day, and after the discussion of some points which they pretended they had not at first understood and after a display of some Afridi by-play generally resorted to on such occasions, agreed to the construction of the road on the 18th September. In return for this they were to receive an increase of Rs. 3,000 to their allowances, of which sum Rs. 2,500 were to be paid to the clan and Rs. 500 as malikana, i.e., rewards to Maliks. On the 19th September they haggled over the distribution of this amount, but eventually agreed to its division as follows:

> Rupees 1,000 per annum to Sherakki and Bosti Khel.
> "  1,000  "  to Zarghun Khel.
> "  750  "  to Akhorwal.
> "  250  "  to Tor Sapar.

Various disputes of a petty nature have also arisen as to the distribution of these sums between the different 'kandis' of the sections, but these one and all have been amicably settled, with the result that the road between the Kotal and Aimal Chabutra has practically been completed and the behaviour of the Afridis has been all this time beyond all praise, for hundreds of outsiders have come to work on the road and have been encamped in tents dotted about all over the pass, and not a man has been touched and nothing stolen. Before finishing this I may mention that the Eastern Hussan Khel, the payment of whose allowance of Rs. 400 is now made by Deputy Commissioner, Peshawar, agreeably to orders contained in Punjab Government letter No. 1386, dated 5th November 1896, put in a claim for a share in the new subsidy. The matter was disposed of in Government of India order No. 26 F., dated 4th January 1900, to Chief Secretary, Punjab, which ruled that they had no claim, and this also disposed of similar claims which were about to be put forward by Daulatzais and Aka Khels, who were only watching to see the result of the Hussan Khel application.

**Antiquities**

The Rajwara lar, the inscription on a large rock at the foot of the kotal, the Shahi Kooi, and the dry well on the top of the Zindan Tara are monuments of the rule of a former people over this tract of country. The Rajwara Lar, or Buddhist road, as the name implies, would seem to have been constructed by Buddhists, and the supporting walls in some portions of the road, still existing, are the relics of the architectural skill of that people.

There is not much to be learnt from the inscription on the rock at the foot of the Kotal. It is quite certain that the inscription was written at a date later than that on which the road above referred to was constructed, for after calling for blessings on the reign of the Emperor Jehangir and proceeding on a panegyric on the powerful and clever Mirza who is responsible for the wording in Persian of the inscription, it exhorts, through one Muhammad Hussein Khan, the brave, loyal and faithful Zainu Khel to keep a proper surveillance of their country and guard their posts. Who Muhammad Hussein Khan was, and who the Zainu Khel are or were, I have not been able to ascertain.

The 'Shahi Kooi' midway in the pass, now filled up by the lapse of time with mud and stones, was presumably named after the same Shah or Emperor, i.e., Jehangir. Afridis can give no information on the subject.

On the top of the 'Zindan Tara' is a dry well into which the Afridis now say were thrown the offenders and criminals of a time when a people called the Dilazak ruled in this country and parts of Peshawar.

**Physical characteristics**

The Adam Khel is physically a tall, strong, broad-shouldered man as a rule. Living in a country which experiences the extremes of heat and cold, they are inured as it were to the rigours of every climate. In the heat of summer they may be seen with a skull cap on driving to and fro between the mines and the pass, their pack bullocks and camels used in the salt trade, and in the same garments in midwinter they are to be found plying a trade in grain, &c., between Kurram and Kohat. Treachery has been ascribed as one of the qualities of the Pass Afridi,* I must say that in my experience of them I have not found them treacherous, and in fact I am rather of the opinion that they are true to their engagements. If they are treacherous at all, they are not more so than the Khaibar Afridi or Orakzai. Courageous and enduring they certainly are, and it seems a matter for regret that they are not more generally enlisted in the Native Army. There is a groundless prejudice against them on account of unreliability. This is more the fault of the manner in which they are enlisted than of any inherent evil in their constitution. Adam Khels are as a rule intermingled in companies of infantry commanded by native officers of the Khaibar Afridi clans. There is a mutual distrust between the

---

*Within the last 10 years I have known of one case in which a Pass Afridi has deserted from the army with a rifle.—D. Donald.

two, and the Adam Khel very soon sees that the Khaibari is not likely to show him up for promotion, and so either leaves the regiment peacefully or very often in doing so takes a rifle as well to spite the native officer. If these men were enlisted as class companies under their own native officers, I am of opinion that they would prove as great, if not a greater, success than the Khaibar Afridi. Avarice is the Afridis' besetting vice, and the Adam Khels like all other Afridis are very prone to it. As regards his hospitable nature he is guided by the maxim 'Ta ta darsham se ba Rake, ma ta rashe se ba Raore,' i.e., when I go to see you what will you give me and when you come to see me what will you bring for me. It is all take and no give. On the whole he is a hail fellow well met, and loves and appreciates a joke.

## How controlled

In my opinion the Pass Afridi of the present day is easy to manage. It has always been known that subsistence for him is greatly dependent on the salt trade. If he is prevented from taking part in this, a source of livelihood is lost to him. In recent years the Passmen at considerable expense and trouble have built for themselves fine and imposing villages which they foresee that in the event of a quarrel with us will be destroyed, and that it will be no easy or inexpensive task to rebuild them. Moreover, there is a good deal of money owing to Pass Afridis by British subjects in the Peshawar and Kohat Districts, and if they misbehave themselves they feel that we can call in this money. They are not at all disposed to fall out with us, but these few facts remind them constantly that a rupture with the Government would not be a paying concern.

## Marriage custom

Their marriage customs are very much the same as those of the rest of the Afghans, except that an Afridi perhaps sells and buys a bride for a little more than the others.

## Hamsayas

The custom of taking in hamsayas is somewhat different amongst the Adam Khels, to that in vogue amongst Tira Afridi and other Afghans. On arrival a hamsaya or dependent, who seeks the protection of a Malik, is feasted together with the whole of his family by the Malik who takes him in. If afterwards the hamsaya should wish to return to his home, he has to give a feast to the entire village in which he has been living. There is only one family of Hindu hamsayas living in the pass, and there are men of Mattanni who live in Akhor. The rest of the hamsayas are mostly abscouded offenders from the Kohat and Peshawar Districts.

## Vengeance re infidelity of wives

The ordinary custom amongst Adam Khels, as well as amongst other Afridis and Orakzais, is to take the lives of two men of the family of which a member has been found to be carrying on a *liason* with the wife of another man. If caught in the act, the man and woman are both killed, and this disposes of the matter for good and all, and no further action is necessary. If, however, the woman has been murdered on good suspicion of her guilt, the aggrieved husband or some other near male relation does not feel that he has been avenged till he has taken the lives of two men of the offender's family. I only know of one case in which a man and woman were killed together in my eleven years' experience of the Adam Khel Afridi. I therefore conclude that they are a moral race of Pathans. The Hussan Khels are somewhat different to the rest of their brethren. In such cases they consider it sufficient to expel the offending man and woman from their country except, unless caught in the act, when the offenders suffer the ordinary penalty.

## Dress

In dress the Gallai and Jowaki resemble the Bangash of the Kohat District, and the Hussan Khel copy the dress of the Khattaks of the Peshawar District, who live close to their border. The old women, however, still adhere to their old Afridi costumes.

## Tip

The Kulla Khels chiefly, but the other sections of Adam Khel as well, are in the habit of cultivating lands known as 'chariker' in the Peshawar District belonging to the Mohmand villages of Adozai, Aza Khel and Mattanni. If the winter rains have been heavy the Pass Afridis flock to these lands and cultivate them. On reaping the harvest the cultivator pays in 'tip' a certain share of the produce. The Kulla Khels who have carried on this system of cultivation for years on fixed fields, in the absence of any mutual arrangements which they may have made with the owners of the soil, have to pay one-fourth of the produce of the fields on barani lands and half on abi. The other Pass Afridis as a rule give such a share of the crop as will satisfy the Mohmand proprietor of the land.

## Jowakis

The first place for numerical strength and power amongst the Adam Khels is generally accorded by the other sections to the Jowakis. The fighting strength of this portion of the clan is variously estimated at between 3,000 and 3,500 men, but the large tract of country over which it is spread, and the great want of cohesion which exists amongst the different sub-sections, renders this strength more or less nominal. For eight months in the year a great part of the Bazid Khel, Mir Bash Khel and Sultan Khel sections are in Maidan (Tira) completely out of touch with the rest of this section of the clan. I have already touched on the migratory nature of these three sub-sections, and that is as much as it is necessary for me to say concerning them, considering that they are in no way important. The rest of the Jowakis, i.e., the resident and stronger portion of them, live in three distinct tracts of the country enclosed in the space above specified as the territory of the Adam Khels. They have homes in the 'Pitao' or Southern Valley, which forms the southernmost boundary of the Adam Khel sphere for very nearly the whole length of the country; they also occupy a table-land enclosed by high hills known as 'Pasta Wani,' and the Bori Valley, which is possibly the best known of the three. These settlements are conterminous. The main strength is located in the Pitao and Bori Valleys, and these afford protection to the weak settlement in Pasta Wani which lies between them.

The Pitao Valley in length from 'Tor Tang' about 5 miles east of the Kohat Cantonment to Bulbulla Khoara, a dry stream which divide the eastern border of the Jowakis from the Khattak village of Khoja Khel, is about 18 miles, and in breadth, on the plain, from Shindand to Jammu its broadest part is about 6 miles. It is more or less an open valley intersected by low hills, the most prominent of which is the low range known as 'Periano Kamar', or the Cliff of Fairies, which divides the villages of 'Paia' and 'Gariba' on the east from the remaining settlements in the valley. Old Jowakis describe this country formerly as being a kind of 'Garden of Eden', whose acres were covered with an abundance of fruit trees and flowers, though a glance of the country as it now exists would leave one in amazement as to how such a change from its alleged pristine virtues could have been brought about. There can be no doubt that the valley has seen better days, and old mounds of stones and mud now mark the sites of once strong and powerful fortifications. Lines of scorched and struggling lime trees in some of the favoured and watery tracts are all that are left of the vaunted fruit gardens. If the winter rains have been sufficient, a visit to the country towards the end of March even now reveals a sea of red, yellow and white flowers—mainly wild poppy, tulips and field lilies. This is the only good which inter-family feuds, the main cause of the destruction of the houses and property of the Jowakis, seen to have done for this people, for with feuds on the increase the clan have had to part with their cattle, and in consequence the flowers alone for a short season are left to an unappreciative folk, there being hardly any cattle, sheep and goats to graze them up. The western end of this valley is occupied by the Keemat Khel with its sub-sections the Kassim and Ismail Khels, distinctly hostile and antagonistic to each other. The rest of the valley is occupied by the Haibat Khels in the centre and the Moghal Khel at the eastern corner.

It is remarkable to note the various histories of these sub-sections.

The Keemat Khel at the western end till within the last four years enjoyed what has become very well known as the Aabari Mushki feuds, the former was head of the Ismail Khel and the latter the head of the Kasim Khel. This feud has been settled,* but it is as likely as not to re-open at no very distant date.

Of the Haibat Khel section the village of Gharibo has been incessantly engaged a feud for the last five or six years. The rest of the Haibat Khel profess to deplore its existence and secretly help in its development and growth with no other object than to see the belligerents reduce themselves to a state of weakness from which they can only emerge as the dependants of the stronger sub-sections of their sections. Again, of the section of the Moghal Khel, the Tattar Khel and Asaf Khel were at it hammer and tongs not more than a year ago, and the Fatteh Khel, the third sub-section, watched with tears and sorrow the settlement of this feud by the intervention of the Deputy Commissioner and the assistance of Malik Akbar, Ismail Khel.** The feud between the Asaf Khel and Tatar Khel seems likely, however, to break out again. The Bori Jowakis excepted, who are generally the peace makers in feuds existing amongst the Pitao Jowakis; the remainder of them seem to be keenly interested in causing disturbances of the peace amongst their own men, and so developing the resources of their country. It is lamentable to see this state of affairs existing among a people who are not only the finest of their class, but one of the most splendid of the Afghan race.

Apart from inter-sectional feuds the Paia or Eastern Jowakis are hostile to the Hussan Khels who live at the eastern end of the Adam Khel country. This feeling originated like most of the others in petty raids and thefts committed by one faction against the other, and culminated in its present uncontrovertible state by the act of the Hussan Khel who about 15 years ago treacherously shot down three or four Jowakis whilst discussing in a jirga a proposed amicable settlement of their quarrel. Since then the parties have

---

*It has lately broken out afresh—D. Donald.
**Renewed about a year ago.—D. Donald.

been approached on one or two occasions with a view to some settlement being arrived at between them, but at a very early stage of the proceedings the hopelessness of such an undertaking is realized by the openly antagonistic feeling displayed by one against the other. Colonel Muir, Commanding the 17th Bengal Cavalry, who has men from both these factions serving in his regiment, some six years ago, with the sanction of the Government of India, requested that some steps should be taken to restore peace and order between them. A move was made, but as aforesaid at the opening stages of the negotiations it was apparent that, unless the Government was prepared to assume great and uncalled for responsibility in the matter of maintaining the terms of a forced and patched up truce, that no satisfactory settlement was possible, and the question had therefore to be postponed indefinitely, and in this condition it remains to the present day. Owing to the Paia Jowakis being themselves embroiled in inter-sectional feud, the Hussan Khel have recently enjoyed comparative immunity from Jowaki attacks, and till the former can settle their own affairs, the latter are content to let matters rest, as they appear so far to have got the best of the quarrel. There appears to be no scarcity of water in this locality, a large number of villages being able to procure abundant supply from wells of an average depth of some 20 feet. Some of the villages in the Ismail Khel and most of those in the Kasim Khel (Shindand) and Moghal Khel (Paia) tract have such wells which not only supply ample and pure drinking water, but are capable of being used for irrigation purposes. The wells in Shindand and Paia assure the occupants of the land in their vicinity of two regular and bumper harvests every year. The Haibat Khel villages of Jammu and Bagh are dependent on the running water of the Nara stream, which, seldom if ever, fails them for drinking water, though in season of draught the Jowakis of Bagh which is below Jammu, occasionally complain that they have not been able to grow joar (Indian corn).

The flow of Nara stream is most erratic at its sources, near Pasta Wani it is mere trickle, near what is known as the 'khoala' or mouth, 5 miles lower down and about a mile and-a-half above the village of Jammu, the flow of water is so abundant as to make it capable of working two water-mills. In this state it passes on to the village of Bagh, below which it has formed two or three deep pools full of small fish. For the next 4 miles not a drop of water is visible till between the Brahim Khel section of the Ismail Khel and the Aimal Khel sub-section of the Kasim Khel pools of water at intervals unconnected by flowing water are again visible. About 2 miles below this point the water again rises to the surface and is again a running stream, filling the large pools after which the villages of 'Shindand' are named; after 'Shindand' the water again disappears for about 5 miles till the village of 'Seab' in British territory, about 2 miles above the junction of this stream with the Kohat Toi at Kotari Machingi, where again it is copious running stream augmented by the water of Gumbat and Kharmatu streams.

## Roads

The main roads through this country are first the high road through centre of the valley between Kohat and Shadipore Police Station, passing the village of Ziarat Sheikh Allahdad. This is a good road, the distance between Kohat and Shadipore being about 26 miles, over which a horseman can canter his horse for three-fourths of the way. There are two entrances at the Kohat end, one by the Tor Tang Pass and the other by Sarra Ghondi. They are both easy, but the latter is quite open and has no physical obstructions of any sort or description. Another road from any part of the Pitao or Southern Jowaki country goes via the Nara Khoala and follows the course of the Nara stream as far as Pasta Wani, and from thence over a low kotal known as the Tangi into Bori and over the Sarghashi Ridge passes the Ashu Khel village of 'Kandao' on to the plain above the villages of Aza Khel and Adozai in the Peshawar District. In 1875 during the temporary closure of the Kohat Pass road, it was seriously considered to open out this route for the salt trade from Kohat to Peshawar, but a lot of work will have to be done on it near the Nara Khoala and on the Tangi Pass between Pasta Wani and Bori, before it is likely to become practicable for camels or mules. Another road, which is frequently repaired by Jowakis to make it practicable for their camels and bullocks used in the wood and charcoal trade with Khushalgarh, passes from Pala and the Central Pitao Jowaki villages near by Bazid Khel and Tandi Jowakis and over the Kuka China Kotal into Talang, and so on to Gumat, Ghorizai and the Khushalgarh. This section of the clan is mainly dependant on the wood and charcoal trade with Khushalgarh for its subsistence. The majority of the Pitao jowaki are engaged in this trade, and large numbers of them, owing to internal feuds, have left their homes and are living in British territory. Hence it follows that when the large part of the population is entirely dependent for livelihood on a trade which they must ply in British territory, and when a large number of their people are resident in British territory, that in our political dealings with the tribe no difficulty of any kind whatever is experienced in making them comply with our demand; not that the Jowakis are in any way people of a vicious or unruly temperament, as a matter of fact they are very much the reverse.

## Pasta Wani

The next Jowaki settlement is that of Pasta Wani, lying between the Pitao Jowaki country and Bori. It is a raised table-land lying between high hills, and consists of some five villages inhabited by a few Kulla Khel and Adam Khel Jowakis. The presence of the Kulla Khel of the Ashu Khel section of Adam Khel is explained by the fact that the country once belonged to that section, and the greater part of the original owners were driven out of it by the Jowakis who now cultivate their lands, the remnant of the Kulla Khels occupying their holdings as the dependent of Jowakis. The men of Pasta Wani are peaceful and quiet, and never give any trouble and seem exceedingly well disposed. On the occasion of my visit to this village with Captain Falcon, 4th Sikhs, then the district recruiting officer, our baggage animals, chiefly donkeys which had that day started from Bagh, got stranded in the 'Nara Khoala'. When at nightfall our tents and baggage had not arrived, the people voluntarily saddled their pack bullocks and brought up our baggage and refused 'bakhshish'. As these men are not in receipt of any allowance from Government, I am of opinion that their action in this case was due simply to their good-will towards Government officials. We spent the night in Pasta Wani, and our tents were watched during the night in heavy snowstorm by the local people of their own accord.

## Bori

With a small account of Bori, which is already fairly well-known, my account of the Jowaki closes. The settlement of Bori in which all sections of Jowakis are represented is an oblong space some 2 miles long and about a mile broad into which are crammed no less than 19 villages or rather hamlets. The land is good and sandy, and is dependent on rainfall for cultivation; but in my experience of ten years I have not known a single year in which the Bori spring crop has failed or been of an inferior quality. The total population of Bori consists of about thousand, and its fighting strength is estimated at about 200 men. The population trades in wood and charcoal with Peshawar and Khairabad, and some of its enterprising members are engaged in the illicit trade in stolen rifles and ammunition. Many of the stolen rifles are said to be brought into the country by traders in wood in Khairabad. These Jowakis occasionally participate with the Paia Jowakis in their feuds with the Hussan Khel, but being neighbours of the latter clan their support of their Paia brethren is, to say the most of it, half-hearted. Bori is an open country and is easily approached from every, except its southern, side; over the Sarghashi Ridge a road made by us is still used by the Jowakis to carry wood on bullocks and donkeys to Peshawar; from the western 'Wuch Algadda' side held by the Kulla Khel the country is open and the road, though commanded by high hills, is not obstructed by physical difficulties. From the eastern or Hussan Khel sides the approach is also easy and unobstructed. The water-supply of these villages is obtained from a spring at the foot of the hills to the south of them and from tanks.

**Political relations**

In 1851 the Jowakis commenced a series of raids on the portion of British territory lying between Kohat and Khushalgarh. In that year Lieutenant Lumsden drew attention to the commission of these offences, some of which had gone as far as attacks in force on Khattak villages. He suggested that Khoaja Muhammad Khan, the Khattak Khan, should be told to make an example, with his 'lashkar' of the villages of Paia and Ghareba, whilst Major Coke with his force kept the Jowakis of Tarkai and Sarkai in check and so prevented any assistance from them reaching the offending villages.— (Gazetteer of North-West Frontier, Volume II, pages 748 and 749).

In 1853 on a representation made by Major Coke regarding a continuance of these raids an expedition was despatched against the Jowakis of Bori, who submitted after their villages had been destroyed. In 1853 the Jowakis, in consideration or assistance afforded us in making their brethren the Gallai come to terms, were granted a subsidy of Rs. 2,000.

This they continued to enjoy till 1877, when for their misconduct an expedition was sent against them which resulted in their complete submission and the forfeiture of their allowances. The terms imposed were:
1) Complete submission in Darbar.
2) Payment of a fine of Rs. 5,000.
3) Permanent expulsion from Jowaki territory of four ringleaders.
4) Surrender of 25 English rifles and 25 matchlocks.
5) Hostages for future behaviour.

'In lieu of the fine, 33 Enfield rifles and Rs. 50 in cash were afterwards accepted.' (Gazetteer of North-West Frontier, Volume II, page 752.)

In 1888 and 1889 the Kasim Khel sub-section, who had afforded refuge to a large number of outlaws, committed several offences in British territory. To punish them Government ordered a secret attack to be made on the villages of Shindand. The attack which took place on 17th November 1889, under the direction of Colonel (then Captain) Leigh, was a complete surprise, and resulted in the capture of Malik Mushki, his turbulent nephews and several outlaws. After spending five years in the Dera Ghazi Khan Jail, Malik Mushki was released and is now a peaceful and respectable man as far as we are concerned.

In 1892 it was suggested that a certain sum was spent in entertaining the Jowaki hostages given to us in 1877, and that it would be more advantageous to allot this sum to the Jowakis as a subsidy and make them maintain four tribal levy towers on their border. The Government accepted the proposal, and the Jowakis were only too pleased that such a suggestion had been made; and from that year they enjoy a subsidy of Rs. 1,848 per annum, which was originally the sum spent in the entertainment of hostages.

## Hussan Khels

The Hussan Khels guard the eastern boundary of the Adam Khel country, and live in a valley which practically forms the western limits of the Cherat sanitarium. In point of numbers they, in their own large family, come next to the Jowakis. This section of the clan has numerous ramifications and sub-divisions, but for practical purposes it is sub-divided into four parts, not counting the Akhorwals who are also Hussan Khel, but who have been dealt with separately in the account of the tract forming Kohat Pass proper and occupied by the Gallai section mainly. These four divisions are named after the name of the locality in which they live. These tracts are Taroonai, Kooi, Janakoor and Musa Darra. Taroonai is at the Peshawar or northern entrance to this valley, and Musa Darra is at its southern exit into the Zeera country. In all this space there are some 28 villages, 7 cach in Taroonai and Kooi, 9 in Janakoor and 5 in Musa Darra. Broadly speaking, Taroonai and Kooi are occupied by the Mian Khel and Zakka Khel sub-divisions of the section and Janakoor and Musa Darra by the Barkai and Tatkai sub-sections. The Pirwal Khel sub-section of the Akhorwals are of the former, and the Gaddia Khel and Bolaki Khel of the latter of the sub-divisions.

The fighting strength of the Hussain Khels is reported to be about 2,000 men, but this is in my opinion an exaggerated figure, and from 1,200 to 1,500 fighting men would be nearer the mark.

In 1893 the control of this section of the Adam Khels was transferred from Deputy Commissioner, Kohat, to Deputy Commissioner, Peshawar, as the Hussan Khels have more dealings with that district than they have with Kohat. In former days they made it their business to be more closely concerned in pass affairs than they are at present; for the possibility of the improvement of the pass road with its concomitant increase in subsidy was a fact ever present in the minds of the Afridis. It is my belief that this transfer of the Hussan Khels to Peshawar simplified the subsequent negotiations for the obtainment of a good military road through the pass in 1899. The previous objections of the Afridis to the road were based more on the amount of profit likely to accrue than to any political dislike of a good highway through their country, and the greater in proportion would the difficulties have become as the numbers of the sharers in the allotment increased.

The Hussan Khels had since 1850 always received from their closely connected brethren the Akhorwals a share of Rs. 400 of their subsidy. This grant was termed 'pasona', i.e., a gift dependent on the good-will of the donor. The Hussan Khels had chaffed at this, and were anxious to make this grant of a permanent nature and to receive it as a recognized subsidy at the hands of Government. In 1862 what are termed the pass internecine quarrels broke out in which the Hussan Khels played a prominent part, in the assistance afforded by them to the Gaddia Khel sub-section of Akhor against the Bolaki Khel sub-section which was helped by the Gullai. These were settled by Major Pollock in 1866, and one of the conditions of the settlement was that the Hussan Khels in future would receive this sum of Rs. 400 out of the Akhor subsidy from Government with the stipulation that they were not to consider themselves in any way concerned in pass management.

In 1899 after the Gullai and Akhorwals had given their consent to the construction of a good road, the Hussan Khels gave in a petition to the Deputy Commissioner, Peshawar, claiming a share in the new subsidy. This petition was rejected by Government; and this order had the effect of restraining the Aka Khel Afridis and Daulatzai Orakzais from submitting similar petitions; for they were only waiting to see how the application of the Hussan Khels fared. Finding this unfavourable the former refrained from petitioning, and the latter have only made verbal demands.

In appearance the Hussan Khels seem to be superior to the rest of the Adam Khels. They are as a rule taller in stature, fairer in complexion and generally of a more comely appearance. This is in a measure due to their wearing apparel which is as a rule cleaner than the rest of their kinsmen. They live close to villages occupied by the descendants of Mian Kaka Sahib who are as a rule easily recognized by their white garments, and the Hussan Khels, as far as possible and where funds permit, copy them in dress. Moreover, a large number of them take service in the Army, specially in the cavalry branch, where they learn to take a pride and pleasure in being well dressed. The reason why Hussan Khels take service in the cavalry instead of the Infantry is said to be due to the fact that they are so following the traditions of their forefathers who had a reputation for being horsemen, who used to raid the fertile valley of Peshawar on horseback instead of on foot.

The Hussan Khels also pay through Government a small share of Rs. 36 odd of their subsidy to a sub-section of the Mohamadis living is Kandao in lieu of assistance received from them in their feuds with the Jowakis.

## The Asho Khel

The Asho Khel are the descendants of Adam by his second wife Asho. They are sub-divided into four sections of which the Kulla Khel are the most important and numerically the largest. Of these an account has been given earlier in the report. It only remains to be added that their (Kulla Khel) fighting strength is about 250 men. When in Tira they, like the rest of the Adam Khels there, are Ghar or Samil in faction, accordingly as the Kambar Khel or Malikdin Khel party is in the ascendent. They are a quiet, inoffensive people, and in customs, manners and appearance are more like the Khaibar Afridis than the Adam Khels of the Kohat Pass. The Mohamadi sections with its sub-divisions, the Rukhan Khel, Mohabati Khel and Hassanbi Khel, lives chiefly in a group of two or three villages at the foot of the hills south of Fort Mackeson known as Kandao. They are better known as the Kandaowals. Their fighting strength is about 150 men, and they receive a small allowance of Rs. 36 odd from the Deputy Commissioner, Peshawar, which was given to them 'pasona' by the Eastern Hassan Khel out of their own subsidy for assistance given to them in their quarrels with the Bori Jowakis. They are permanent dwellers in Kandao, and the several sub-sections are all embroiled in blood feuds.

The Ali Khel section of some 50 fighting men live in two villages near Kandao known as Kandar.

The Khairadin section consisting of the Preedai and Pakhai sub-sections live in seven small villages which lie between the Kulla Khel settlements in Wuch Algadda and the Jowaki colony in Bori.

D. Donald,
Commandant, Samana Rifles and Border Military Police
Kohat.
6 May 1901

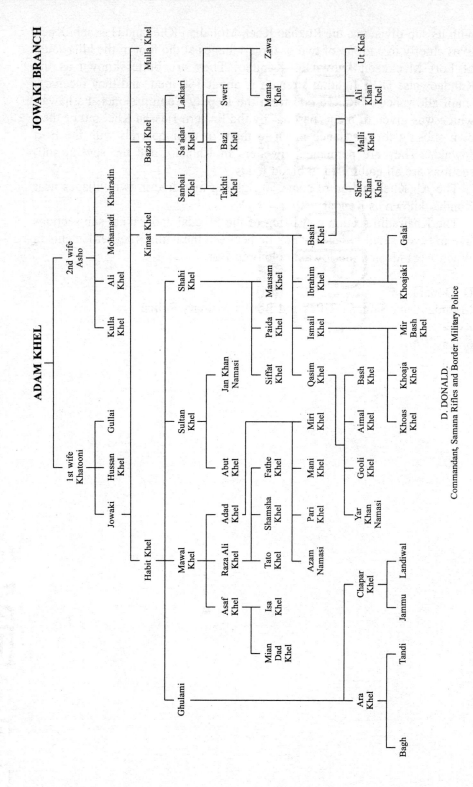

JOWAKI BRANCH

ADAM KHEL

D. DONALD.
Commandant, Samana Rifles and Border Military Police

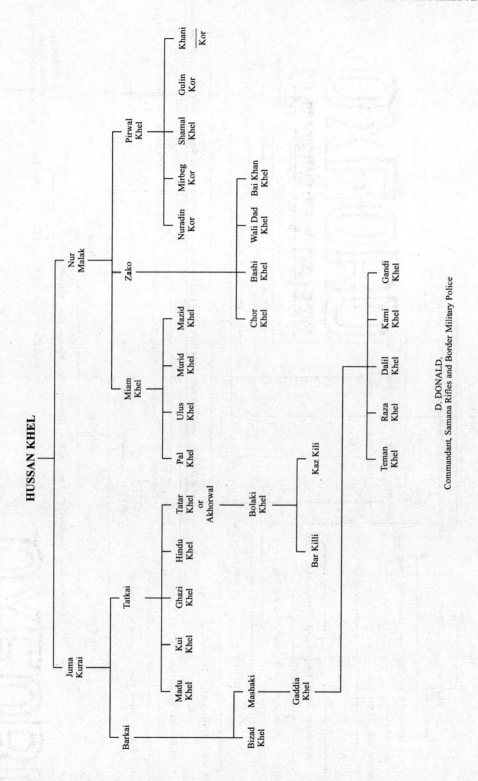

## HUSSAN KHEL

- Nur Malak
  - Pirwal Khel
    - Nuradin Kor
    - Mirbeg Kor
    - Shamal Khel
    - Gulin Kor
    - Khani Kor
  - Zako
    - Chor Khel
    - Bashi Khel
      - Wali Dad Khel
      - Bai Khan Khel
  - Miam Khel
    - Pal Khel
    - Ulus Khel
    - Murid Khel
    - Mazid Khel
- Juma Kurai
  - Tatkai
    - Madu Khel
    - Kui Khel
    - Ghazi Khel
    - Hindu Khel
    - Tatar Khel or Akhorwal
      - Bolaki Khel
        - Bar Killi
        - Kaz Kili
  - Barkai
    - Bizad Khel
    - Mashaki
      - Gaddia Khel
        - Teman Khel
        - Raza Khel
        - Dalil Khel
        - Kami Khel
        - Gandi Khel

D. DONALD.
Commandant, Samana Rifles and Border Military Police

89

**GALLAL**

Khawa

Said Ali

Hassan Ali (Husseni Khel—Sooni Khel)

Yar Ali — Shir Ali — Yaghi

1st wife Zarghuna — 2nd wife Dama

Kachai (Zarghun Khel) — Yaral Khel Shapalkiwal

Sarfaraz — Muhamad Khel — Sardar Kor — Sarfaraz Kor — Yar Mohamad

Darwesh Kor — Miri Khel — Sher Zaman — Hakam

Dilbar Kor — Biyaz Kor — Najum

Karam Sher — Shir Zaman — Karam Sher

Mughal — Karam Sher

Muhammad Yar Kor — Gul Khan — Momand

Tura Baz Kor — Unus Khel — Kadar Khel — Azad

Dara Shah Kor — Munda Khel — Fateh Kor — Mauzam Kor

Sahib Sher Kor — Malak Kor — Musa Kor — Miru Kor

Akhel — Mian Din — Pastu — Azam

Qasim Khel — Malla Khel — Zaman Kor — Miri Khel

Boi — Umraz — Ayaz — Shir Baz — Gul Zadah

Malang — Azmat Kor

Nazar — Jabbar — Sardar Khel — Shah Baz — Mughal

Yar Gul Kor — Makhmad Kor — Tash Khel — Tura Khel — Landi Khel — Aimal Khel — Sanghar

Misri Khel — Zafar Khel — Karam Sher Kor — Madsher Kor — Ram Sher Kor — Gul Sher Kor

Saleh Kor — Arsala Kor — Aziz Kor

Bosti (Bosti Khel)

Firoze — Abubakar — Baqal Khel — Alam Khel — Janal Khel — Shamal Khel — Nizam Khel — Abubakar Khel — Attak

Surkan — Sarwar Khel — Hindugi — Bakhtu Khel — Surak

Ghowegawar — Gul Shah Kor — Firoze Kor — Mir Kor

Gulzar Kor — Mir Khan Kor — Mansur Kor

Astu (Sheraki) — Khadi — Dharma Khel — Mubarak Khel — Bash Khel

Afzal Neka — Mulla Neka

Malang — Mazid Khel — Bazid Khel — Sherin — Aziz Khel

D. DONALD.
Commandant, Samana Rifles and Border Military Police.

Конат:
The 6th May 1901.

## Subsidies and their distribution, Kohat Pass.

| Sanction | Amount | Distribution | | | | | | Remarks |
|---|---|---|---|---|---|---|---|---|
| | | Bosti Khel | Sherakki | Tor Sapari | Zarghun Khel | Shpalkiwal | Akhorwal | |
| Government of India, Foreign Department letter No. 653 E., dated 20th September 1882. | Rs. 5,000 | Rs. 475 | Rs. 475 | Rs. 950* | Rs. 950 | Rs. Nil | Rs. 2,150 | *Tor Saparis pay a one fourth share of this to Kooiwals. |
| Government of India. Foreign Department letter No. 653 F., dated 20th September 1882. | 660 | 240 | 240 | – | 120† | 60 | – | † This is 'dâk' allowance; Rs. 60 per annum are paid to Malik Sattar, son of Ghulam. The other Rs. 60 are paid to Maliks Feroz, Noaze and Ulassi. |
| Punjab Government No. 20C, dated 12th October 1899, to Commissioner, Peshawar. | 3,000 | 500§ | 500§ | 250§ | 1,000‡§ | – | 750 | ‡ After deducting honoraria of Rs. 40 and Rs. 20 for Sooni Khel and Shpalkiwal and Rs. 120 granted to the three Mohamad Khel Maliks above mentioned, balance is divided into four equal shares.<br><br>§ One sixth of these sums are deducted for payment to Maliks as lungis or rewards. |

The 3rd May 1901.

D. DONALD,
*Commandant, Samana Rifles and Border Military Police.*

91

## Distribution of Jowai subsidy

| Sanction | Amount | Keemat Khel | | Haibat Khel | | Remarks |
|---|---|---|---|---|---|---|
| | | Ismail Khel | Kasim Khel | Haibat Khel or Mawal Khel | Moghul Khel | |
| Government of India, Foreign Department, No. 1216 F., dated 23rd june 1892 | Rs. 1,848 | Rs. 462* | Rs. 462* | Rs. 462 | Rs. 462 | * Ismail Khel and Kasim Khel give a one-fifth share of their subsidy to the Braham Khel which is an intermediate section between the two. |

The 3rd May 1901.

D. DONALD,

*Commandant, Samana Rifles and Border Military Police.*

Punjab Government Press, Lahore — 10-7-01 — 100.

# Index